CREATING AND PRESERVING WEALTH

By

C. Foster Stanback

Creating and Preserving Wealth
Copyright © 2011
Foster Stanback

Cover design by Jonathan Stanback

All rights reserved. No part of the publication may be reproduced, stored in a retrieval system, or transmitted to any form or by any means—electronic, mechanical, photocopying, recording, or otherwise—without the prior written permission of the author and publisher. The only exception is brief quotations in printed or online reviews.

Published by Lulu®
www.lulu.com

Printed in the United States of America

ISBN-978-1-105-09881-9

Acknowledgements

This book would not have been possible without the unique education I received from my father. Family members have told me that when he was a young boy, he received a train set and an encyclopedia for Christmas. He quickly abandoned the train and proceeded to read the encyclopedia, which he found far more interesting. Eventually, he would read it all the way through. This episode gave a clear signal of how he would spend a considerable portion of his life as an adult. Though he became very successful as a businessman and investor, he eschewed the common "toys" that many wealthy people purchase to entertain themselves with, opting instead to make reading his primary pastime. He read about everything: history, science, business, economics, politics, etc.

My brothers and I have been the beneficiaries of his great quest for knowledge. When we were very young, he began telling us all sorts of interesting things about the world we lived in. One of his favorite sayings, which he repeated to us over and over, was that "a man who won't read is no better off than a man who can't read."

To make sure we got the point, he would constantly give us books. In the beginning the books were fictional—the great tales about epic sea voyages, pirates, and the Old West. Later, he laid the heavy stuff on us—*The Wealth of Nations* and *The Intelligent Investor*. Then the articles began, a relentless stream of them that he had culled from reading through dozens of business and news publications. He had already done the hard work of sifting the wheat from the chaff, so all we had to do was digest the choice kernels that he had provided for us. Rather than give us long lectures about the world of business and investing, his approach was much more subtle, relentlessly exposing us to the right ideas.

For decades he sent those articles, week after week, year after year. Then he learned to use email and the flood really began. Like the work of the waves against the rocks on the seashore, he gradually shaped our thinking and inoculated us against so many of the false notions that abound in the business world.

Since I have three boys of my own, I desperately wanted to convey to them the wisdom that my father had passed on to me. Yet I realized that I had neither the talent nor the discipline to reproduce his unique teaching model. It is my hope that this book represents the next best thing, a highly condensed version of some of the most basic principles that should guide our financial thinking.

In addition to my father, Fred Stanback, I would like to acknowledge my two older brothers, Brad and Lawrence. They not only began their tutelage before I did, they were also much less distractible pupils. Whenever I have had a question or an idea, they have always been there to answer my questions and clarify my thinking.

Educational endeavors are always a creative process, as facts and principles are interpreted within an ever-changing historical context. I am certainly a product of my times and have done my best to make the correct application of what I have learned. Some of the ideas that I have presented in this book may need to be altered as circumstances change. Nevertheless, it is my deep conviction that the principles upon which they are based are timeless.

Table Of Contents

Chapter 1
Introduction
9

Chapter 2
How Wealth Is Created
15

Chapter 3
Work
23

Chapter 4
Skill Development
31

Chapter 5
Scaling Up Production
39

Chapter 6
Threats To Stored Wealth
43

Chapter 7
Vehicles For Storing Wealth
79

Chapter 8
Conclusion: The Future Of Wealth Creation In America
131

Chapter 1

Introduction

In short, the way to wealth, if you desire it, is as plain as the way to market. It depends chiefly on two words, industry and frugality; that is, waste neither time nor money, but make the best use of both.

—Benjamin Franklin

Almost everyone who has traveled to the western United States is familiar with the ubiquitous Carl's Jr. fast food chain. Founder Carl Kartcher began the business back in 1941, pushing a small hot dog cart that he purchased with a $311 loan and $15 cash from his wife's purse. From these humble beginnings, he was able to capitalize on the increasing accessibility of the automobile and the growth of American suburbia. He established an extensive chain of restaurants that could provide quick meals for a public on the go.

Although his burger empire never rivaled that of legendary McDonalds founder Ray Kroc, he nonetheless became fabulously wealthy over a period of several decades. He knew the fast food business well—how to provide a product that customers wanted, how to market it, and how to maintain operational efficiency and profitability.

He was also a man who exemplified the values of hard work, simple tastes, and giving back to society. These qualities would almost certainly have propelled him to ever greater levels of prosperity were it not for one bad decision made back in the 1990s. Seeing an opportunity to parlay his enormous wealth into an even larger fortune, he decided to bet everything he had—and then some—on a commercial real estate venture. He leveraged his bet with large loans that he was confident could be paid back once he had cashed in.

Unfortunately, things didn't turn out as planned. The commercial real estate market took an unexpected plunge and Karcher ended up with $71 million in debt. Although his attorney urged him to declare bankruptcy, he refused and spent the rest of his life paying off what he owed.

Carl Karcher's story exemplifies many lessons that will be expounded upon in this book. From his early days, it can be seen that wealth creation is not easy—it requires tremendous dedication and consistent hard work, often doing something unglamorous like selling hot dogs from a pushcart. This timeless principle is conveyed to us by the ancient writer Epictetus, who tells us how Lampis the ship owner, on being asked how he acquired great wealth, replied, "My great wealth was acquired with no difficulty, but my small wealth, my first gains, with much labor."

Kartcher's pushcart also teaches us other important lessons about wealth creation—that it is usually surprisingly simple at its core and that it is better to start off small with a minimum of investment and risk rather than embark upon complex ventures that involve large amounts of capital.

Of course, there are always exceptions, and just about all of us would like to be one of them—the person who wins the lottery, the aspiring actor who gets discovered and becomes a movie star, or the lucky entrepreneur who makes millions on a new idea. Although popular culture reinforces the belief that anyone can achieve such success if he or she perseveres, reality is unfortunately far different. Statistics show us that wealth is elusive for most of the world's population—even those that are talented and hardworking. Most business ventures fail—in spite of the zeal of the founder. And most investments are risky and result in a loss of capital. Those that aren't usually provide only an average return.

This rather bleak reality has proven unpalatable for countless numbers of people, causing them to seek out quick and easy pathways to prosperity. There has been no shortage of peddlers and practitioners eager to meet this widespread demand. Selling products from books to software programs and offering to let people in on their money making "secrets" at pricey seminars, they lure people into empty "get rich quick" schemes.

Even those who have already attained great wealth can be just as vulnerable, falling prey to corrupt money managers who seem to possess magical powers for generating high investment returns. And their methods really work—until they stop working, that is. Of course, no one really knows beforehand whether the large gains are the result of a Ponzi scheme, or luck, or a perfect match between a manager's methodology and a particular set of historical circumstances that will eventually change.

In spite of claims to the contrary, no one has ever discovered a way to consistently generate great wealth. But the formula for creating relative wealth is simple and straightforward. Relative wealth is the wealth you can attain relative to the financial position you will most likely be in if you do not implement certain practices. That is, any one of us can become wealthier than we otherwise would be by following a few simple principles and learning to recognize and avoid the common financial traps that ensnare so many people.

Chapter 2

How Wealth Is Created

There is not, never has been, and never will be any substitute for productive work. No amount of legislation, no amount of money, borrowed or coined, no economic prestidigitation, governmental or otherwise, can, as such, increase by one iota the wealth of a nation or the standard of living of a people. Existing wealth or property can be and is being redistributed by law, but new wealth can be created only by men and by the man-made machines they guide.

—Philip D. Reed

In modern industrialized countries the process of wealth creation is often obscured by numerous stages in the production process and a complex system of intermediaries. Further complexity is added by a vast array of financial instruments derived from the real economic activities themselves. Much of this financial activity creates friction rather than lubrication for the wheels of commerce. Furthermore, it clouds peoples' understanding about how wealth is truly created and channels their energies and capital into a quagmire from which escape is difficult or impossible. The financial industry has generously provided it's own guides who—for a fee—will happily offer their services to lost travelers. But more often than not, they only lead people deeper into the morass of their own making.

A return to the simplicity of an earlier era can give us a clearer picture of how wealth is created. Indeed, this process hasn't really changed at it's core since the dawn of civilization. Once they had advanced beyond a hunting and gathering society, our earliest ancestors began to produce wealth in four simple ways. They grew food crops and raised livestock. They collected or dug up raw materials such as wood and copper. They manufactured items such as tools and weapons. And they provided services to each other, such as healing or performing religious rites.

The foundation of our modern economy really hasn't changed after all these years. Food production, raw materials, manufacturing, and services still sustain human societies. Every working individual earns a living within one of these sectors, although he or she may be many steps removed from the actual product or service being sold.

In capitalist societies the majority of products and services also have markets that determine their selling price. Eventually a normal price range is established. If someone offers to sell at a lower price, he will probably be able to sell more of it. Likewise, if he raises his price, he will sell less—or none at all.

Apart from the actions of the seller, prices for various goods and services are ultimately determined by their desirability and scarcity within a particular society. Regional variations in scarcity and demand also form the basis of trade, so that goods and services that are abundant in one area can be exchanged for scarce goods and services that are abundant in another area. Thus, Saudi Arabia trades it's abundant oil resources for engineering services and manufactured goods.

Basic economics has important implications for individual wealth creation. Most people must make a living by offering their skills for sale in the labor market. They usually end up receiving compensation that falls within a normal range for a particular skill. Highly developed and scarce skills typically command a higher price than skills that are widely available or easily learned—a doctor earns more than a fast food worker.

Thus, the conventional pathway for creating wealth in most societies involves a long and arduous educational process to develop the most highly remunerated skills. In general, those that attend the best universities land the best-paying jobs, depending upon the discipline they choose to study. Business, law, medicine, and engineering are usually the top paying professions. Without a doubt, some talented artists, musicians, and actors can often earn much more, but as a profession those that offer these skills to society usually receive less than those in the previously mentioned disciplines.

Those who are born into families that own businesses can often avoid the rigorous academic pathway of wealth creation. In their case the vehicle that produces the wealth already exists and they simply inherit it. Alternatively, they may inherit capital in the form of financial instruments such as stocks and bonds that can be liquidated and channeled into a new enterprise. However, without the management skills acquired from a lengthy apprenticeship, success is unlikely.

As with any of the principles described in this book, there are exceptions to the aforementioned generalities. Yet for anyone desiring to improve his ability to create wealth, seeking to understand the exceptions will be a fruitless endeavor. Practical human knowledge has been accumulated empirically, either through trial and error or through the systematic application of methodologies such as the scientific method to a particular problem. The result is the identification of a particular cause or causes for a certain effect. In the case of wealth production (relative wealth, that is) a number of causes can be identified with a fair degree of certainty. It therefore follows that if these causes can be replicated, wealth creation should ensue. Exceptions are just that because even when the suspected causes are replicated, wealth does not always follow.

For example, it is universally recognized that maintaining a healthy diet, exercising, and getting plenty of rest will improve a person's chances of avoiding illness and living a longer life. Nevertheless, there are some people who blatantly defy these practices and yet still manage to avoid the consequences.

How they can achieve such a feat remains a medical mystery. For some people, drinking alcohol, smoking, eating fast food, and avoiding physical exertion are pleasurable experiences. Those inclined toward such a lifestyle would no doubt like to learn the "secret" of the few who have managed to live this way without serious health repercussions. But the secret remains elusive. When offered the conventional wisdom, they may counter that even those who try to live a healthy lifestyle may suffer from serious illnesses and die young.

Thus, there are exceptions on both sides—the reckless reveler who lives to a ripe old age without ever visiting a hospital, and the young athlete who dies of a heart attack. But for the person who wants to be proactive and actually do something to better his chances of good health and a long life, the conventional wisdom prevails. Indeed, it is the only approach bolstered by the collective experience of many generations and the extensive data from modern medical research.

So wealth creation is in principle no more complicated than the health advice of a good country doctor. Work hard, improve your skills, spend less than you earn, and invest the proceeds in safe financial instruments. As Albert Einstein said, "Make everything as simple as possible, but not simpler." This formula should serve as the litmus test for any wealth generation vehicle. If it seems too simple or too easy, it probably is.

One must also be careful not to err on the other side of Einstein's equation by making the process of wealth creation seem so complicated that only a theoretical physicist—or a Harvard educated money manager—could ever hope to understand it. High net worth individuals often fall into this trap. Complexity is erroneously equated with low risk and high returns—a combination that violates one of the most fundamental rules of finance. Complexity does not amplify the value created from basic economic activities. It merely obscures risk and creates a dangerous dependency on experts and "trusted financial advisors."

Chapter 3

Work

Labour was the first price, the original purchase-money that was paid for all things. It was not by gold or by silver, but by labour, that all wealth of the world was originally purchased.

—Adam Smith

The basic input for wealth creation always has been—and always will be—work. Human energy must be expended to produce something that was not there before. Wealth arises from the surplus of production—whatever is not immediately consumed. Once again, it is helpful to return to the simplicity an earlier era to gain a better grasp on this principle. Primitive peoples worked primarily for food—their very survival was always at stake. If they could somehow produce more food than they consumed, the surplus could be traded for other goods that would enable them to further increase production (tools, seed, etc.). Or, they could trade for goods that would improve their comfort and well-being (clothing, the services of a healer, etc.).

Before the Lydians invented coins in the 7th century B.C., wealth was measured by the extent of one's land holdings, surplus goods that had been accumulated, or rare commodities, such as gold or gems. Once coinage became a proxy for value, people could also store their wealth in this new medium. About 1500 years later, the Chinese invented paper money. Although this new monetary instrument made business transactions much more efficient, it proved to be a poor means of storing value. Governments tended to print too much of it to cover their expenses and the value of the notes was eroded by the resulting inflation.

Stored wealth—whether it is in the form of land holdings, livestock, coins, or paper money—has always been the source of capital. Capital can be invested in an existing business enterprise to expand capacity (thereby generating even more surpluses—and greater wealth), or invested in a new venture. Alternatively, it can be loaned out to someone else in exchange for interest payments. Eventually, markets emerged where people could buy and sell partial ownership interests in businesses (shares of stock) or documents representing a legal obligation to pay back a loan with interest (bonds). Thus, stocks and bonds became additional financial instruments in which value could be stored. But the underlying source of the value was, in most cases, the human labor that had been expended.

In the case of a commodity like gold, the labor to find it and extract it is a major component of its value. Thus, a commodity that is easier to find and collect (such as sand) is worth far less. There are certainly other sources of value apart from labor inputs. Gold, even if it were abundant, would still probably be coveted because of its perceived beauty. Some works of art, such as a Picasso or an Andy Warhol painting are extremely valuable because of certain attributions that our modern culture has attached to them.

Sometimes, enormous labor can be expended without producing any value at all. An eccentric old woman that the author once knew as a child expended tremendous energy producing things that had great subjective value for her, but none whatsoever for other members of society. She once took a number of old turkey wishbones and created little characters with them, which she carefully placed in a diorama to portray a bizarre storyline that she entitled, "Turkey Trot." In spite of the many hours she put into the project, it is doubtful that it ever could have been sold for any amount of money. Her heirs would more likely have had to pay someone to get rid of it after her passing. Fortunately for them, it burned up in a house fire.

Certain services may have a high value in one culture and no value in another. Thus, a witchdoctor may receive a relatively high compensation for his services in an isolated jungle community, but probably would not fare very well in a modern industrialized nation (Oddly enough, this trend seems to be changing). Economists continue to debate how value is created, but it can safely be said that labor inputs combined with societal attributions are at least an important factor for many products and services.

The financial instruments that human societies have created can be likened to the honey produced by a hive of bees. The honey is a store of energy that can be accessed by the bees in the winter when their normal food source is not available. It is derived from the activity of many bees working day after day to collect and process nectar. Once the bees begin to consume it, the store of energy will steadily decline and will need to be replenished through renewed labor in the spring.

Like honey, financial instruments store the value derived from human labor. They can be utilized for temporary sustenance when work activity ceases. But they also have the potential to be self-sustaining to a certain extent. When they represent a claim on an income generating entity such as a business, a property from which rents can be collected, or a bond that pays interest, it is possible to passively acquire additional wealth without the input of work. Most people labor throughout their lives to achieve such a state in retirement. Accumulating an asset base that is large enough to be self-sustaining (generating enough income for the owner to live on without eroding the initial value) usually requires many years of consistent saving.

Many people, especially those whose work is difficult or monotonous, are eager to shorten the time they must wait in order to enjoy passive, labor-free income. To speed things along they can be seduced into gambling their accumulated savings in an attempt to generate unusually high returns. It must be remembered that returns are positively correlated with risk—the higher the returns, the greater the risk that must be taken to generate them. The correlation is probabilistic. That is, occasional exceptions may occur, but in the vast majority of cases, the rule holds true. A low return with high risk is also quite possible, as many hedge fund investors have discovered to their great dismay.

Some people, inspired by stories of famous entrepreneurs, plunge headlong into their own business ventures. More often than not, they fail and lose their life savings in the process. Starting a business should be a natural progression from working for many years within a particular field. Technical knowledge, as well as familiarity with costs, suppliers, and markets can then be leveraged to form a new enterprise that will have a reasonable chance of success. But without this knowledge and experience, starting a business is a very risky endeavor. Statistics show that new business ventures have an eighty percent failure rate.

Thus, the only truly sound approach to creating personal wealth is to work hard and to keep working over an entire lifetime. The process of accumulation can be sped up considerably by developing greater skills within one's chosen trade, or to develop the new skills necessary for a better paying job.

Chapter 4

Skill Development

Do you see a man skilled in his work? He will serve before kings; he will not serve before obscure men.

—King Solomon (Proverbs 22:29)

Skill can be acquired through education and training accompanied by practice and experience within a particular field. Education entails academic preparation; that is, reading and study. Training involves frequent interaction with other individuals who are already proficient at the skill you wish to acquire. By observing, asking questions, and soliciting input from others, abilities can be improved.

Practice means actually doing the thing you are learning about and observing. The experience gained through this practice allows you to develop knowledge that cannot be obtained by reading and study alone. Malcom Gladwell, in his tremendously popular book *Outliers*, discusses research indicating that achieving a high level of proficiency in any particular skill requires 10,000 hours of practice. If this is the case, then those who wish to command a higher salary should seek employment within a field that offers opportunities for advancement, then remain there for many years. Shifting from job to job will make it impossible to acquire the specialized knowledge and refined skills that will lead to a higher salary.

However, if it becomes increasingly evident that the particular skill set you have acquired over many years is becoming obsolete, then it is better to make a decisive leap into a new field of work and begin the process of skill development all over again. Delaying this step will only result in a prolonged period of anxiety and financial misery.

Mark Cook was a brilliant computer programmer. Raised and educated in South Africa, he came to the United States during the 1980s to look for work. He was 27 years old and brought with him only two suitcases. Because he was an expert in one of the most advanced programming languages used on mainframe computers, he soon landed a job with a Wall Street investment banking firm. He often worked late into the night alongside a group of smart, hard-driving MBAs who needed his technical expertise to implement their ideas. And he was well-compensated for his services.

But eventually things began to change. Networked personal computers started to replace mainframes, bringing with them a whole new generation of highly-trained job seekers. Mr.

Cook soon became a "dinosaur" in the fast-changing world of computer programmers.

Fortunately, he was able to land a new job at NASA. Though his monetary compensation decreased considerably, he at least had the satisfaction of doing work that was interesting and meaningful. Eventually however, even NASA decided to "get with the times" and upgrade their computers. Mr. Cook once again found himself without work—and now he had a family to support.

After considerable searching, he was able to find employment with the power company—a last refuge for those with a "prehistoric" technical skill set. But this particular utility happened to be located in another city that was four hours away. Unable to move his family, he had no choice but to commute for a week at a time, living in a motel and returning home only on weekends.

When this arrangement became unbearable, Mr. Cook finally decided to set out in an entirely new direction. Leveraging his technical abilities, he sought out training in the field of project management. Eventually he started teaching courses in this field through an online university, though the pay was rather low. Finally, however, he was able to land a well-paying job as the project manager for a large insurance company.

Mr. Cook's story had a happy ending. But unfortunately, many people never embrace the urgency of continually upgrading the skills they can offer to the job market. This situation is especially disheartening among blue-collar workers. The news always seems to be filled with stories about skilled workers in heavy industries such as autos and steel that suddenly find themselves out of work. Their prospects for once again receiving the high wages that they had known for so long are all but impossible in the new job market.

Many of the factory workers in traditional industries are the legacy of the scientific management practices developed by Frederick Taylor in the late 1800s. Taylor sought to improve labor productivity by eliminating waste and standardizing the most efficient practices. Complex tasks were broken down into their simplest components so that the applied skill of the worker was minimized. As a result, factories were no longer dependent upon individual craftsmanship to produce a final product. Less efficient (or more expensive) workers could easily be replaced. Eventually they were, either by machines or by cheaper laborers found overseas. Taylorism greatly increased the efficiency and profitability of American industry, but it also eroded the power of workers over their employment destinies.

Disenfranchised workers often seek a political solution for their condition, banding together and putting pressure on elected officials to implement some structural change in the economy. They often find inspiration in the ideas of philosophers, sociologists, and economists who cite the flaws inherent in the capitalist system. Over the years, these thinkers have offered numerous permutations of an alternative socialist model for economic prosperity.

Though many aspects of the socialist economic model are indeed appealing, all societies must eventually face the Darwinian reality of competition for scarce resources. In such a world, unjust as it may be, only the fittest will survive. Plants and animals that were better adapted to their environments, through drought resistance, better hunting capabilities, etc., ultimately survived while their counterparts died out.

Collectively, it is certainly a noble and worthwhile endeavor to create a more equitable society in which everyone can enjoy stable employment and a good quality of life. Perhaps the solution lies in some optimal mix of components from the capitalist and socialist economic models—a formula that we have yet to discover. Winston Churchill claimed that "the inherent vice of capitalism is the unequal sharing of blessings; the inherent virtue of socialism is the equal sharing of miseries." Until this tension can be resolved in some new economic system devised by future generations, we must work with what have. Admittedly, the current system leaves much to be desired, but to quote Churchill again, our present system, like democracy, is "the worst system devised by the wit of man except for all the others."

Individuals desiring to increase their relative prosperity should therefore adapt to the environment they currently find themselves in. Channeling one's energies into finding a political solution for economic ills will be a slow and uncertain pathway to achieving greater wealth.

Chapter 5

Scaling Up Production

The prudent, penniless beginner in the world labors for wages for a while, saves a surplus with which to buy tools or land for himself for another while, and at length hires a new beginner to help him. This is the just, and generous and prosperous system which opens the way to all, gives hope to all, and consequently energy, and progress, and improvement of conditions to all.

—Abraham Lincoln

When a person has achieved a high level of skill within a particular field of employment, better wages will usually follow, opening up the possibility for faster capital accumulation. This prospect will of course depend upon the discipline and frugality of the worker. All too often, surplus funds are frittered away on more expensive material goods in an effort to duplicate the lifestyles of wealthier people in the community. Even those who have committed themselves to living below their means can be enticed by the constant barrage of advertisements that assail us from every front. The government itself colludes in this process, prodding us to spend all that we have and even take on debt in order to prop up an ailing economy that is overly reliant on consumer spending.

But the true road to prosperity for any nation and its citizens is for each person to save as much as possible, then invest his or her accumulated capital in enterprises that produce needed goods and services. Individuals who have developed a skill that is in high demand can use their savings to expand their productive capacity by hiring and training others to work for them. In this way they will be able to meet the market demand and achieve greater profits while simultaneously helping others along the pathway toward greater skill development.

The surest way to grow a new business is to move slowly. Incremental additions of personnel and equipment will allow an entrepreneur to maintain better operational control over a budding enterprise while others within the organization are prepared for greater management responsibilities. Moving slowly and methodically will also lessen the need for large infusions of capital.

Even when a person has developed sufficient technical and managerial skill to launch a business and hire employees, he should never commit all of his capital to the new venture. If it fails—and many do despite the best of efforts—he will have no reserves left to take care of other needs, such as medical emergencies, retirement, etc.

Sadly, many people become so enthusiastic about their businesses that they commit all of their financial resources to the cause. Some even take on a considerable amount of debt to see things through. Such errors are reinforced by "rags to riches" lore and stories about entrepreneurs who "went for broke" and later reaped the rewards of their total commitment. But the stories about all those who "went for broke" and actually ended up in this state never make the bestseller list—unless they repeat the process and get lucky the second time around. Unfortunately, most people never succeed in business and never make a comeback after the first round of losses.

Chapter 6

Threats To Stored Wealth

It requires a great deal of boldness and a great deal of caution to make a great fortune, and when you have got it, it requires ten times as much wit to keep it.

—Ralph Waldo Emerson

The wealth that has been accumulated from a lifetime of labor must be guarded very carefully. As seen in the case of Karl Karcher, the perfect mix of youthful energy and being in the right place at the right time in history cannot be reproduced later in life. In rare cases, people who have lost everything they have worked for are able to leverage their accumulated wisdom to take advantage of a new opportunity, minus the youthful energy. But lightning seldom strikes in the same place twice.

The "honey" that has been stored in the summer of one's youth will be needed during the winter of one's old age. People who rely on their children to take care of them are only drawing away from the surplus that their offspring would otherwise accumulate for their own retirement. Thus, a never-ending cycle can be created that saps the resources of grandchildren and great grandchildren. In many parts of the world, the imperative for children to provide financially for their parents dooms successive generations to never ending poverty.

In a well-known Bible passage, Jesus Christ urged his followers: "Do not store up for yourselves treasures on earth, where moth and rust destroy, and where thieves break in and steal" (Matthew 16:19). His primary purpose was a warning about the perils of greed, but these ancient threats to accumulated wealth are still quite relevant today (if moths and rust can be interpreted in a metaphorical sense).

Following this line of thought, the three greatest dangers to one's savings are thieves (nothing much has changed here, except the evolution of thieves into the white collar variety like Bernie Madoff). Moths quite literally destroyed peoples' wealth by laying eggs in their woolen clothing, which was a significant investment for the average person. Thus, moths are the perfect metaphor (a tapeworm also works well) for money managers and financial advisors, who seek to lay their eggs in their clients' portfolios and reduce the value of their returns through high fees. Rust gradually destroyed iron tools and weapons, which often represented a considerable outlay of capital. For our purposes here, rust is an excellent metaphor for inflation, which gradually eats away at the value of peoples' savings.

Thieves

In the modern era, the traditional thief has a very limited ability to inflict devastating financial losses. Most people store the majority of their wealth in a non-physical form such as bank accounts, stocks, and bonds; or, in physical assets such as homes or land that can't simply be carted away. Even high value items that can be stolen, such as jewelry and electronics, are usually protected by a homeowners insurance policy. Although a burglary can certainly cause a financial setback, most people will completely recover within a short time—provided, of course, that they were prudent and kept their insurance up to date.

But victims of financial scams suffer a far more devastating fate. As the Bernie Madoff Ponzi scheme so clearly demonstrated, people can be completely wiped out financially virtually overnight. Nancy Silverton began her career as a chef at only 18 years of age. While she was a student at the California State University in Sonoma, she began working as a cook in the dormitory. She soon became so passionate about cooking that she decided to abandon her degree program in political science and travel to London to attend the world famous Cordon Bleu school for chefs. After completing her training, she returned to California where she began working as the assistant pastry chef in a high end restaurant.

Eventually, she accumulated enough funds to open the La Brea Bakery, which she founded in 1989. The business was so successful that she later expanded her production facilities to serve wholesale clients. After many years of hard work, she decided to sell the bakery in 2001 for $5 million. She could now slow down her frenetic pace and focus on smaller restaurant ventures, knowing that she had plenty of money for retirement and for her children's education.

Since she was more interested in cooking than in dealing with finances, she decided to procure the services of a prominent Beverly Hills money manager named Stanley Chais. As it turned out, Chais was achieving remarkable returns by handing over his client's funds to an even better manager—Bernard Madoff. These high returns were so alluring that, against the advice of her father, Nancy decided to place everything she had into Chais' hands.

For the next few years, her decision seemed to be working out very well. She received a regular statement showing that her nest egg was continuing to grow far faster than that of other investors using more conventional vehicles. But then one day in 2008, she received a phone call from her father (who by this time had also invested in the fund). He told her that they had lost everything.

Madoff's enormous scam was not just limited to wealthy clients who invested millions of dollars. By using various feeder funds that channeled smaller investors' money into his hands, he was also able to destroy the life savings of many average working people. Louis Kelsch and Robin Lieberman worked their entire lives as public school teachers. They were always very frugal, even avoiding such luxuries as cable television and discretionary home repairs.

But thanks to a tip from Kelsch's father, a New York City firefighter, they found a way to speed up the long, slow process of wealth accumulation. They invested their savings with Madoff at the very early stages of his scam. For more than twenty years, they faithfully deposited their meager savings into Madoff's investment fund and watched it grow like magic. Finally, they retired from their jobs in the Ohio school system, knowing that they had a solid nest egg. They would at last be able to make a few of those long-needed home repairs. But then, like thousands of other investors, they got the news that their accumulated savings had completely vanished.

Although Bernie Madoff was able to achieve the largest take in the history of financial scams, his methods were by no means unique. He simply combined some of the classic tactics that have always been used to separate overly trusting people from their wealth. The real engine that drove his scam operation was nothing more than a Ponzi scheme—that is, using funds from new investors to pay off those who had invested previously, leading them to believe that the proceeds were actual profits from the operation. Charles Ponzi, who immigrated to the United States from Italy in the early 1900s, was so adept at this scheme that his name became attached to it, but the method itself is very old. Charles Dickens even mentions it in a novel he wrote in 1857.

A Ponzi scheme is by nature quite simple, so it must be disguised in order to get people to buy into it. The most common tactic is to pack the proposal with arcane financial jargon and appeal to the expertise of extremely savvy money managers who have special inside knowledge that they can capitalize upon. Although some sort of profit-generating mechanism is mentioned, how it actually works is so unfathomable that prospective clients give up trying to figure it out and instead rely upon their instincts about the person promoting the investment.

Such instincts usually boil down to whether or not they perceive the perpetrator of the scam as friendly and likable, which they usually do. Unfriendly con artists will almost certainly have to find another line of work, possibly in the "back room" of some illegal operation, but not dealing with clients face to face.

Shady money managers rely heavily on image management, and can often dupe people by displaying the material trappings of success. A friend of the author who is a successful business owner once pointed to the high end sports car driven by his financial advisor as evidence of his expertise in choosing investments. Although (so far) there was no evidence that this advisor was engaged in any wrongdoing, squandering $200,000 on an asset that would quickly depreciate in value was a clear sign that he was a person controlled by his amygdala rather than his pre-frontal cortex. What business did he have telling people how to manage their finances?

Others, despite their personal penchant for luxuries, deliberately tone things down. Like chameleons, they can change their colors as needed to blend into the environment of their targets. One middle-aged scam artist carefully cultivated his image to appeal to wealthy senior citizens. Knowing that many of them were conservative, he realized that fancy Italian suits and sports cars would immediately elicit distrust. Instead, he drove a large American car—a black Cadillac—and wore dark, conservative suits when he met with his clients. After convincing an elderly couple to turn over all of their financial affairs to him, he went on a personal spending spree with their checkbook before he was finally caught and thrown into jail.

Many of us would like to think that we are, as the line goes, "a pretty good judge of character." But we can all be deceived at times. Rather than rely on our imprecise instincts, we will fare much better if we are guided by sound principles. One such principle that is often quoted in financial circles is: "If it sounds too good to be true, it probably is." Promises of high returns with little or no risk are by nature quite hollow. Another principle, heard less often because of the large number of individual practitioners working in the financial industry, is: "Never entrust the management of all of your wealth to a single individual." This principle should be followed religiously—no matter who the person is, who recommended him, or how gifted with a Midas Touch he happens to have been in recent years.

These principles will be readily grasped by most people, as they are based on simple common sense. But unfortunately, common sense can easily be short-circuited by greed. Greed is a very powerful drive that exists within all of us. We can often resist greed when we recognize it as such, but we are just as often deceived. Greed can disguise itself as altruism, making us think we don't want to acquire wealth to indulge in material pleasures, but rather to have more funds available to do good works for others. However, our time and energy is probably a much better gift to society, and we will have none of it left if we lose all of our accumulated wealth and have to spend the rest of our lives working long hours just to survive.

An equally powerful drive within us is the desire to feel important. This drive is often fueled by events and circumstances that in the past made us feel inferior or inadequate. Achievements or recognition from others compensates for this void and we therefore have a strong tendency to seek these things out in the various ways that our society provides them.

Status symbols are one of the most common means for satisfying the need to feel important.

This mechanism has existed in all human societies since ancient times. Archaeologists can determine the wealth of a long-buried household by studying the refinement and artistic embellishment of various articles that have been left behind. The actual utility of such items is usually no different from that of their humbler counterparts in poorer homes. But ancient people who had accumulated greater wealth typically liked to display it with more ornate pottery, tools, art objects, and clothing.

Modern manufacturing methods have eliminated many of the quality differences stemming from individual craftsmanship. Companies therefore rely on clever marketing strategies to create a perceived value difference in the minds of customers. At their core, such strategies seek to tap into the deeply rooted desire people have to feel important. By connecting their products with a lifestyle that is exclusive and highly coveted by the majority of people, they can brand them as items that merit a much higher price.

Many wealthy people, like their ancient predecessors, find it very difficult to resist the status appeal of certain material goods—especially clothing, jewelry, and cars. Those who can exercise greater self-control will accumulate wealth at a much faster rate. However, there are other status symbols which non-physical in nature that can be even more compelling. Gaining admission to exclusive social circles has a very powerful allure for most people. Sophisticated thieves can use this urge to great effect to consummate their scams. Bernie Madoff created opportunities for larger investors to mingle with the rich, famous, and powerful at country clubs, galas, and other events.

The tactic was extremely effective and provided excellent re-enforcement for his scam. Most people, like a school of fish, assumed that there was safety in numbers. Rather than expending the effort to study how his investment vehicle actually worked, they took a short cut and just assumed that many of these other wealthy, smart people would have already done that difficult work. Thus, as long as one remained within their company, the investment was safe.

Moths

The financial industry has been extremely successful at convincing people that trying to manage their own savings is foolhardy. Slick advertisements and well-crafted articles in business publications tout the expertise and sophisticated techniques of top-performing investment funds. The ideology they promote seems reasonable on the surface—delegate investment management to the professionals while you continue to focus on running your business or making money in your career. The guild of money managers works hard to present their trade as being a necessary specialization, just like doctors, lawyers, and accountants. The value added for customers is the higher rate of return that can be obtained by placing funds with these practitioners.

But money management is fundamentally different from other trades. A top neurosurgeon can be relied upon to deliver the same level of performance year after year. Luck and historical circumstances have little bearing on outcomes. Though many money managers make the same claim, the evidence shows that their assertions are simply not true.

For decades, the stockbrokers were the most powerful gang on the Street. They would hit people up for commissions on their purchases and sales of securities. They could usually do quite well for themselves, and the large financial firms that backed them always got their cut. If they managed to gain the trust of their clients, they could often convince them to continually buy and sell in the hope of cashing in on market fluctuations. Over time, however, information exposing this practice of "churning" became widely disseminated and more and more investors could spot the scam. Once online trading accounts became available and "discount brokerage" went mainstream, the profits from trading stocks (both for the brokers and for the financial firms) were drastically reduced.

Conditions were ripe for the emergence of a new cartel. The money managers who eventually took over the Street found that charging their clients "protection money" was a far more lucrative business. Wealthy individuals and institutions were asked to hand over all of their assets, but were given assurances that it would be kept safe and that they would receive a good return. In exchange, the money managers took their cut, which was usually a percentage of the total value of the assets. Some of the more aggressive managers eventually decided that they wanted more—they wanted a percentage of the total assets on an annual basis (typically two percent) and in addition they wanted twenty percent of any profits. These exorbitant fees eventually became standard within the hedge fund cartel.

The funds recruited bright young talent from America's top schools, luring them away from careers in science, engineering, and medicine with generous cash bonuses and a variety of perks. Within a few years, they could start funds of their own and join the ranks of America's newest social class—the ultra-rich. The previous system of social stratification had a giant middle class, a large number of upper middle class professionals, and a moderate number of wealthy and poor people at both ends of the spectrum. But this structure was quickly collapsing, and the best way to avoid sinking into the impoverished hoards was to sellout to the financial industry. Hard work and loyalty would ultimately be rewarded with a ticket to get into the exclusive club of those residing at the top.

The lucrative business model of the money managers has even been adopted by many financial planners. Traditionally, these professionals provided a useful service in exchange for an hourly fee. They could evaluate a person's personal finances and offer helpful recommendations about investments, insurance, and tax strategies. But for many, the temptation to heist their clients' entire net worth proved too great. Why settle for a one-time fee when it was possible (and often fairly easy) to convince people that they needed to hand over all of their assets?

Perhaps peoples' willingness to comply stems from some deep psychological need to feel taken care of—an inner child seeking a proxy for a wise and caring parent. Or, maybe it's just a desire to be free from pressure and responsibility. No doubt, having a personal money manager is a status symbol for many, a sign to others that they have achieved sufficient financial success to warrant the services of an expert. But those who hand over their wealth to a person or institution to manage it are taking a huge risk and will pay an enormous price for the convenience. When a person is incapacitated or parents want to establish a fund to take care of their children, such a decision will be unavoidable, but it should be made only after considerable research. Any firm that will be given such a trust should have demonstrated its worthiness and financial strength over many years. Going bust and receiving a handout from the federal government should result in an immediate disqualification.

Rust

Anyone living in the post World War II era has noticed that, over the years, everything tends to go up in price. This phenomenon is now considered quite natural and unavoidable. But the experience of previous generations of Americans was very different. Except for brief spikes during wartime and the occasional increases for certain scarce goods, the prices for most items that were commonly purchased had remained relatively stable during most of the nation's history.

Though we have now accepted inflation as a normal part of life (and the government even makes strange assertions about the need to increase inflation to some targeted level), we naturally wonder why it must inevitably occur. There are several reasons. Sometimes opportunists will raise the price of something when it becomes scarce and there is insufficient competition. Price gouging of this sort (especially when it occurs after some destabilizing event like a hurricane) is greatly looked down upon by society. Therefore, those who engage in this practice will sabotage any prospects for building longstanding relationships with customers. They may make some quick profits, but then they'll need to leave town.

Prices can also be driven upwards when some underlying cost goes up which increases the amount that a seller must charge in order to make a profit. For example, when the price of oil goes up, virtually everything else will eventually follow suit. The transportation cost for delivering goods to the stores where customers shop, as well as the increased energy costs to run the store, must inevitably become embedded in the price of the items being sold.

Price increases stemming from these first two causes are generally temporary, although the growing scarcity of oil threatens to bring on a more permanent era of steady price increases. But the most significant (though far less obvious) reason for the continuous inflation occurring since the mid-1940s has been an increase in the money supply. Economists often refer to this root cause of inflation as "too much money chasing too few goods." To understand the dynamics of this phenomenon, it will be helpful to take a brief survey of the history of money.

For thousands of years people exchanged goods and services for the things that they wanted—a practice known as bartering. Although the system worked, it was inefficient: How many chickens add up to a cow? And once you figured this out, you had to carry all those chickens over to the marketplace and hand them over to the owner of the cow.

Around 600 B.C., an ancient Near Eastern people known as the Lydians began using little bits of electrum (a naturally occurring alloy of silver and gold found in the local river bed) as a medium of exchange. Someone could sell chickens to an interested buyer for a few lumps of electrum and then hand these over to the owner of a cow to make a purchase.

To make things easier for everyone, the Lydian king decided to stamp his seal on similarly sized lumps of electrum so that people would know they were getting the proper amount of the metal for a given exchange. Later, the king started pressing these lumps into round discs and the first coins were created. No matter how badly the king wanted to create more money, he simply couldn't do it until he had the electrum to start with.

Other countries saw what a good idea the Lydians had stumbled upon and started minting their own coins out of various metals. The Romans, with their large empire, eventually minted more coins than anyone else. The highest value coins were made out of gold. Lower value coins were made out of silver, and the lowest value coins were made out of copper or bronze. Soldiers were typically given a small silver coin called a denarius for a day's wages.

Sometimes, though, the emperors ran out of money to pay their armies. But they eventually came up with fabulous idea to solve this problem. Why not mix the expensive silver, which was extremely limited in supply, with much cheaper copper and then stamp it into a denarius? Then they would have a lot more money to spend. This process became known as debasing the coinage.

The idea worked for a while, but soon people started figuring out that their coins didn't have nearly as much silver in them as before. Everyone from shopkeepers to gladiator school owners started raising their prices so they could get their fair share of silver in exchange for the goods and services they were providing. Eventually, everyone began to feel the effects of price inflation and the economy was thrown into chaos.

The emperors found out the hard way that their magical method for creating money had a terrible downside. The cure of debasing the coinage to compensate for financial shortages turned out to be worse than the disease. The only way to get prices back under control was to put the correct amount of silver into each coin, even though it meant that the emperors would have less money to spend.

Unfortunately, institutional memory turned out to be very short. Over the centuries, numerous spendthrift emperors and kings emerged who decided to repeat the same experiment, but it always had the same result. Debasing the coinage resulted in excessive inflation.

Then, in the tenth century, the Chinese came up with a radically new innovation: paper money. The concept was surprisingly simple, and since the Chinese had invented paper nearly a thousand years earlier, it is surprising that no one tried it sooner. The Chinese emperors issued paper currency that had a certain value printed on its face. Technically, these notes represented real amounts of metal coins for which they could be exchanged at any time. But no one considered this necessary, since they were backed by the good faith of emperor himself and everyone within the Chinese empire was happy to accept them as a form of payment.

Eventually, however, the government ran into hard times. Armies needed to be paid and the money simply wasn't there. Once again, the same old experiment was tried, but now with a new twist. Money to pay the troops (and buy goodies for the emperor) could simply be printed. And unlike metal coins, who would know? There would not be any distinguishable difference between the paper notes backed by metal and the notes backed by thin air.

At first, the magic worked. Now it seemed as if the emperor could have unlimited amounts of money at his disposal, and all he needed to create it was cheap paper and ink. But then, strangely, prices started creeping upward—slowly at first, but then faster and faster as all of these bills became absorbed by the limited number of goods and services available in the marketplace. The rapidly increasing prices gobbled up peoples' incomes and savings, throwing the whole economy into complete disarray. Sadly, the emperors had to go back to their original idea of making sure each paper note was backed by a sufficient quantity of real metal. The convenience of paper, however, was here to stay.

But half a world away, the same experiment was just getting started. Like gunpowder, this fantastic innovation from the Far East seemed destined to launch European kings to new heights of power. Imitating their Chinese counterparts, kings soon started issuing currency that wasn't backed by gold and silver. Within a short time, economic chaos ensued. From time to time, different rulers repeated the experiment, but it didn't take long for everyone to figure out that simply printing money was a pathway to poverty instead of a pathway to wealth.

This insight led the eminent French scholar Voltaire to claim in 1729 that "Paper money eventually returns to its intrinsic value—zero." But another Frenchman was quick to see an amazing application of this principle—not as an easy means to national prosperity, but as a devastating weapon of war. During his campaigns in Austria and Russia during the early 1800s, Napoleon printed vast quantities of counterfeit notes and unloaded them in these nations, wreaking havoc on their economies. Napoleon, who was as adept at imitation as he was at innovation, was not the first to use printed counterfeit bills as a weapon of war—nor would he be the last.

In 1470 Duke Galeazzo Sforza of Milan counterfeited the money of Venice in an attempt to ruin the rival city-state's economy. When Frederick the Great invaded Poland during the Seven Years War of 1756-63, he flooded the country with counterfeit money. During the American Revolutionary War, the British took all of the cannons out of the warship *Gabriel* and fitted it with a more insidious weapon—printing presses. They anchored the ship at the mouth of the Chesapeake River and churned out large quantities of *Continentals*, the new currency of the aspiring nation. Long before illegal drugs would become popular, the British hired Tory "pushers" to go out and unload these bills in commercial centers like New York City. Even though the Americans eventually won the war, their economy was almost completely ruined by these counterfeit notes. For years afterward, citizens would use the expression "not worth a Continental" for anything they considered to be of low value or inferior quality.

Americans had such distaste for paper currency that the U.S. government didn't even print any again until the Civil War. Some private banks had begun issuing their own currency before the war, and when people had confidence in the strength of the bank, they were willing to accept the convenience of these paper notes, knowing that at any time they could be exchanged at face value for an equivalent amount of gold or silver coins. But war was expensive, so much so that the governments of both the North and the South began printing paper money to pay for military hardware and soldiers' wages. For its nearly valueless currency to have any chance of success in the marketplace, the U.S. government realized that it would need to wrest away the right of private banks to issue their own notes, so all private currency was outlawed at the beginning of the war. It was replaced with the notorious "Greenback" bills throughout the course of the conflict.

Once the smoke had finally settled, these Greenback dollars were plunging in value. In a rescue attempt, the government began issuing silver and gold certificates that could be readily exchanged for actual metal. Public confidence was restored, and the growing prosperity of the nation allowed the government to keep its promise to its citizens—for a time.

In spite of the clear historical evidence that printing too much money led to hyperinflation, the temptation to engage in the practice was just too great for certain governments facing financial difficulties. Following World War I, the Weimar German Republic was bankrupted by the enormous war reparations it had to make to the allies. To get out of the hole, they started printing money. As the resulting inflation spiraled out of control, their government issued larger and larger bank notes in an effort to keep up. In 1921 the exchange rate was 60 German marks to the dollar. By late 1923 the rate had soared to 4.2 trillion marks to the dollar. Inflation was so great that whenever workers were paid they had to rush to the store to buy the goods they needed before the prices went up. Shoppers had to carry cartloads of nearly worthless bills just to buy the day's groceries.

Eventually the notes became completely worthless and people started returning to a barter economy, even buying admission to the circus with things like sausages and cheese. Useless marks littered the streets and were swept away with the rest of the trash. Some used them as fuel for their stoves. The German people became so desperate that they were willing place their trust in Adolf Hitler, who promised to rescue them from their economic misery.

The United States, as a victor in the First World War, celebrated a period of unprecedented prosperity and excess. But the party ended when the stock market crashed in 1929 and the nation plunged into the Great Depression. As people lost their jobs in factory closings and their savings in bank collapses, many of them started hoarding gold, a tactic that had been repeated throughout history during times of economic turmoil. This practice always undermined the financial power of existing governments, and was always repressed with varying degrees of force. During the French Revolution, the Communist Revolution in Russia, and the Nazi Regime in Germany, citizens could actually be executed for owning gold. Such an extreme punishment was deemed necessary to prevent people from switching to another medium of exchange when paper currencies were becoming increasingly worthless because of hyperinflation.

As the Great Depression wore on and the coffers of the United States Treasury became depleted, President Roosevelt decided to grease the nation's printing presses and decouple the dollar from its link to gold. To prevent the widespread hoarding that was already underway, he issued an executive order making it illegal for U.S. citizens to own any form of gold coins or bullion, except for certain coins held by collectors for their numismatic value. Americans had thirty days to turn in any gold they owned, or face a $10,000 fine and a felony charge with 10 years in prison.

Many wealthy citizens circumvented the new law by transferring their gold holdings to Switzerland. Eventually, the government addressed this problem. In 1959 President Eisenhower made it illegal for Americans to buy gold overseas. A few years later, in 1963, President Kennedy made it illegal for any citizen to store gold in foreign accounts.

Even though inflation steadily increased during the post-WWII years, it did so in lockstep with spectacular prosperity and U.S. dominance of the global economy. As American business thrived, more and more people channeled their savings into the stock market to take advantage of the high returns it could provide. Gold as a safeguard against inflation lost much of its appeal among investors. A strong global demand for dollars and adequate revenues from taxes finally prompted the government to abandon its restriction on private gold ownership. In 1971 President Nixon signed an order that once again allowed Americans to buy the shiny yellow metal.

Within a few years, as a response to the high inflation of the 1970s, demand for gold increased dramatically, sending its price to historical highs. But by the 1980s, inflation finally subsided to manageable levels and the price of gold dropped considerably. Over the next few decades, the stock market prevailed as the most lucrative place to store accumulated wealth. Returns above 15 percent were not uncommon. Inflation remained subdued in the low single digits.

In 2008 the United States plunged into a severe financial crisis, the likes of which had not been seen since the Great Depression. The financial industry, as well as the auto industry, had to be rescued with large infusions of government funds. Since the government did not have the money to begin with, it had to be created.

In the 21st century, it is no longer necessary to produce more money by printing it. Rather, it is created digitally in accounts at the Federal Reserve. The U.S. Treasury, which has to sell bonds every week to come up with the funds to run the government, offers them for sale at auctions. If there are no purchasers at the offered interest rate, the Federal Reserve may step in and make bond purchases to keep the rates low. Otherwise, the bonds would sell on the auction floor at a lower price, effectively raising their interest rates. This would in turn make it more expensive for businesses to get loans, leading to a slowdown in economic activity. Thus, money is created out of thin air when one branch of the government (The U.S. Treasury) sells bonds to raise funds, while another branch of the same government (The Federal Reserve) buys them with money that it has digitally created.

As we have seen, the process of money creation has always produced severe inflation and only exacerbated the economic difficulties that led a nation to follow such a policy to begin with. Unfortunately, the age-old lesson is usually lost on every new generation of policy makers that must face the difficult choice between raising taxes and cutting spending, or just printing the money needed to pay the bills. As recently as the Viet Nam War, the United States produced vast quantities of counterfeit North Vietnamese and Laotian currency, then dropped the bills from the air over enemy territory in an effort to wreck the economies of these countries.

Surprisingly, however, the United States government is now attacking its own territory with this same weapon of economic destruction. The reality of what is happening is usually not grasped by the public at large—until it is too late. The very name "quantitative easing" (the preferred government term used to describe the practice of creating money out of thin air) is often a sufficient deterrent to prevent most citizens from prying into the grisly details of monetary policy. Even those that are more curious can quickly become disoriented by the cacophony of economists arguing among themselves.

John Maynard Keynes, the Depression Era economist who became famous for recommending government spending during financial crises, recognized the inherent danger of printing too much money: "There is no subtler, no surer means of overturning the existing basis of society than to debauch the currency. The process engages all the hidden forces of economic law on the side of destruction, and does it in a manner which not one man in a million is able to diagnose…" Covering expenses by printing money (or creating it digitally) can indeed work for a short time, but it is like sailors lost at sea quenching their thirst by drinking salt water. There may be some temporary relief, but death will soon follow.

The most recent country to experience such a disaster is Zimbabwe. The currency of this African nation is also called the dollar. On January 1, 2001 one hundred of them were equivalent to one U.S. dollar. After a decade of unbridled money printing, it now costs 100 billion Zimbabwe dollars to buy an egg. The populace, desperate to find some means of exchange that will hold its value, often digs into the banks of rivers and streams in hopes of finding a few bits of gold.

Fortunately, the United States has not experienced the terrible hyperinflation now occurring in Zimbabwe. There are several reasons for this temporary good fortune. Until very recently, the U.S. government had shown more restraint in its money creation policies. As already pointed out, there is a lag time before the effects of this practice become pronounced within the national economy. Secondly, other countries are doing the same thing. No nation's currency is backed by gold anymore. Value is determined in the marketplace and is measured in terms of other currencies. Thus, a dollar is worth a certain amount of Euros or yen. Any currency can be exchanged for another and will fetch a higher amount depending on how traders view the country's political and economic prospects.

For a time, Iraqi dinars printed under Saddam Hussein's regime were worth something in the global currency marketplace. Now, of course, they are worth nothing. Unlike Hussein's dictatorship in Iraq, the United States government is not going to disappear anytime soon. So the dollar will still be around. People who live in countries that are unstable politically or economically—such as Zimbabwe—want to get their hands on a currency that is more secure. Thus, there is still a worldwide demand for U.S. dollars in spite of their diminishing underlying value. Furthermore, the prices of many commodities around the world—from oil to valuable minerals—are typically quoted in and can only be purchased with U.S. dollars. Foreign banks also hold them as their "reserve currency." For now, the words of Cullen Hightower still ring true: "America has the world's best money. Every U.S. dollar is secured by the universal demand for it."

But circumstances will almost certainly change, as they did for every other great power that once dominated the world economy. Greece, Spain, Portugal, and Ireland are now bound to the euro and cannot simply print more of them to cover budgetary shortfalls. Like the United States, these countries must also offer bonds for sale to generate the funds to run the government.

Unfortunately, much of the money generated must be used just to pay the interest on previously issued bonds. Less and less is available to meet current expenditures. Any buyer of such bonds will understandably demand a higher interest rate to compensate for the added risk that these countries will default on their payments. No one would buy such bonds if it were possible to obtain the same interest rate from bonds issued by a more financially stable country such as Germany. More indebted countries (just like more indebted individuals) must therefore pay a higher interest rate to get loans. As a country becomes more indebted and less likely to pay, it must offer rates so high that much of its revenues are channeled into interest payments instead of services for its citizens. Inevitably, the standard of living in such nations will decline as the government raises taxes and cuts social programs.

The United States is now faced with this dilemma. The weekly requirement for new funds far outpaces the demand for bonds issued by the Treasury Department. Without any sort of government intervention, the price of Treasury bonds on the open market would reflect this slackened demand, resulting in a lower sales price and higher interest rate. Buyers of U.S. bonds—especially nations like China—are becoming increasingly nervous about the possibility that the United States will not be able to meet its financial obligations. This concern would normally be reflected in the sales prices of U.S. bonds, except that the Federal Reserve steps in and buys large quantities of them to prop up the prices and keep the interest rates low. The inevitable reduction in government services and steady decline into a lower standard of living is temporarily avoided. Unfortunately, the rising prices resulting from money creation ultimately have the same result.

Wages almost never rise fast enough to keep up with inflation, so that an ever greater portion of peoples' paychecks goes toward basic necessities. Little disposable income remains for discretionary purchases or savings. Even money that has been saved will steadily lose its purchasing power. Interest rates are unlikely to keep up with rapidly increasing inflation. To use the sailors lost at sea analogy again, any money that is stored will be like fresh water placed in a leaky container.

The monetary policies of the United States in recent years have virtually assured a future of steadily increasing inflation. Even if policy changes are enacted to reduce this trend, the nation still has an enormous debt that will have to be paid. Inevitably, it will be paid through higher taxes and reduced services—which will result in a lower standard of living for most people. The alternative is to keep creating money from nothing to pay the bills, a policy that will inevitably lead to higher inflation and, again, a lower standard of living for most people. Productive citizens who have managed to accumulate some wealth will therefore need to be very careful in deciding which vehicles they will use to store it.

Chapter 7

Vehicles For Storing Wealth

If you're an investor, you're looking at what the asset is going to do; if you're a speculator, you're commonly focusing on what the price of the object is going to do, and that's not our game.

—Warren Buffett

There are four primary vehicles for storing wealth, which the investment community refers to as asset classes. They are stocks, bonds, commodities, and real estate. Many other things are often marketed as investments, but they are not. If the definition is taken at its simplest, then anything that goes up in value over time can be said in retrospect to have been an investment. But for practical purposes this definition should be refined to those things that can be said to have a reasonable probability of going up in value over time. Distinguishing these things from those which have only a possibility of going up in value over time will help show the difference between a sound investment and one that is speculative.

Making this critical distinction is both an art and a science. The artistic component lies beyond the scope of this book, but the scientific component can be elaborated upon. One element that should be analyzed is how a particular investment will increase in value over time. Growing scarcity coupled with increasing demand is certainly a factor that is very likely to make something increase in value. Thus, petroleum, if one had the means to store it cheaply, will probably be worth more in the future than it is worth today. But nothing, of course, is certain. If another cheap, carbon-free energy source becomes readily available, petroleum may be worth nothing at all and even become illegal to use.

Understanding how something will supposedly increase in value can expose the faulty logic built into the marketing of products that are sold under the guise of being good investments. For example, some popular artists today own galleries in exclusive shopping malls. Although their original works are very expensive, they often sell a limited number of high quality copies that, though still pricey, are much more accessible to the average person entering their stores. If prospective customers show even the slightest interest in a particular painting, they are quickly ushered into the viewing room where the painting is placed on a stand and exposed to halogen lighting that is dimmed and brightened to highlight the painting's dazzling colors. Though it might be beautiful, and perhaps even a good accessory for a customer's home, many people will question whether or not it is worth it to pay so much money for a pretty object that has no utility.

To smooth over this resistance, salespeople tout the investment value of the piece, claiming that copies of similar paintings have drastically increased in value in recent years. One that may have been purchased for several thousand dollars, for example, is now worth twenty thousand dollars. The customer is left with the impression that buying a copy of the new painting is not just an impulse, but a wise investment decision. What most customers don't ask, however, is how they would go about selling their painting if they ever chose to do so. The gallery, understandably, would never provide this service, as it must continually make room for the artist's new creations. The reality is that the customer will have to market the painting on his own, selling it on eBay or Craig's List or leaving it in a consignment shop. Although it might eventually sell, it will almost certainly not provide anything like the return described by the salesperson at the time of purchase.

So how can these galleries legitimately make a claim that their pieces suddenly became worth more? Because the gallery itself raises the price to create an artificial increase in value that is completely internal rather than market based. In other words, after selling a few copies out of a limited series, the gallery can start increasing the price by ten percent, twenty percent, thirty percent, and so on. The last few paintings may become so expensive that they never sell, but that is not important. Sufficient profit will already have been made on the previous sales. What is most valuable to the gallery is to convince a few customers to buy the first issues of a painting. By gradually raising the price as each one is sold, they can tell the next customer that the value keeps going up, creating the illusion that the item is an investment. But the price is not being driven up by demand from an external market—it is driven up by the artist who keeps arbitrarily raising it.

There are indeed many original paintings, art objects, antiques, coins, and other collectables that steadily increase in value over time. But only an avid collector who has acquired extensive experience will stand a good chance of identifying an item at the right price to assure a reasonable return in the future. Eclectic collecting for investment purposes is unlikely to generate returns that are comparable to more conventional vehicles.

Stocks and Bonds

In industrialized nations stocks and bonds have become the most widely used means of storing accumulated wealth. Stocks, in general, have historically provided higher returns than bonds, but they are also considered to involve a greater risk of principal loss. The conventional investment wisdom has usually recommended a balanced mix of stocks and bonds in one's portfolio. A popular formula states that a person's age is a good guideline for the percentage of a portfolio that should be held in bonds. Thus, a person who is 30 years old should allocate 30 percent of his portfolio to bonds and 70 percent to stocks. A 70-year-old should reverse this allocation, keeping 70 percent in bonds and only 30 percent in stocks. The rationale is that a younger person can better withstand a loss of principal than an older person, since he can keep working for many more years to replace it. An older person, on the other hand, will have fewer years to work (if any at all) and will depend upon interest payments for retirement income. A loss of principal could be catastrophic.

In spite of its widespread acceptance within the financial community, the truth of this conventional wisdom is questionable. In the short-term, stocks are indeed more likely to decrease in value, resulting in a loss of principal if the investor sells them. But in the long-term, companies and even government institutions can default on their bonds, which also results in a loss of principal. For many years, General Motors was considered to be one of America's finest companies. Many people (including those who worked in the auto factories), purchased the company's bonds with the idea that the interest payments would provide a secure income for them in their retirement. But when the company declared bankruptcy in 2009, these bondholders were completely wiped out.

Municipalities that sell bonds to build schools and roads can also go bankrupt. Although these government entities can create revenue through their taxing power, it is sometimes not enough to cover the city's financial obligations. Currently, many cities and states have enormous debts that they cannot possibly pay back. They continue to issue bonds in an effort to stay afloat, but at some point they will face inevitable collapse. When the music stops, anyone holding these bonds will not be able to find a chair.

Even the bonds issued by the federal government (Treasury Bills) are questionable. Traditionally, Treasury Bills were considered to be one of the safest investments in the world. The United States government, it was believed, could never default on its bonds because it could always just print more money to make good on the interest payments. Yet, as seen in the preceding section, unbridled money printing leads to excessive inflation. Even the federal government can end up between a rock and a hard place so that any policy it implements will result in economic disaster. And the first casualties will be the bondholders. If the government defaults, they will watch their savings disappear overnight. If the government keeps printing money, their meager interest payments (along with their principal) will be eaten up by inflation.

Even when economic conditions are stable, interest payments from bonds almost never keep up with inflation, resulting in a gradual erosion of the bondholder's principal. Some investors may seek to circumvent this problem by investing in bonds that pay a higher rate of interest. Yet by doing so they are drastically increasing their risk of complete loss, as only the most desperate companies and governments are willing to pay above average interest rates to lure investors into purchasing their bonds. Thus, even though this assertion will be hotly contested by many financial professionals, bonds are a poor investment for any individual interested in preserving his or her wealth.

Stocks, provided they are the right stocks, are far more promising. But that, of course, is the rub. Finding the right stocks can be extremely difficult. Yet it does not have to be. Investors who are willing to adhere to the right philosophy and engage in some basic analysis may find that the process is relatively easy. The right philosophy is quite simple to grasp, but unfortunately quite difficult for most people to adhere to.

As Warren Buffett has so often preached, stocks are simply ownership shares in companies—real economic entities that employ workers and make products and services to sell for a profit. If they are well managed and there is demand for the things that they sell, they usually make money. Whatever money is left over after all of the salaries and other expenses have been paid will go to the owners of the company. When there is more than one owner, each one will receive an amount of money commensurate with his percentage of ownership interest in the company (a dividend), as reflected in the number of shares he holds.

Sometimes a company may elect to withhold some or all of its profits and use them to expand the business in the expectation that even greater profits can be made in the future. The owner or owners may be very happy to forego present income for the prospect of more income down the road. When shares of the company they own are available for sale in the stock market, prospects of future growth in income can be reflected in higher share prices. Thus, owners gain a sense of satisfaction as they watch the value of their holdings go up. They realize that at any point they could sell their shares and that even though they did not receive income payments from the company's profits, they could make money from selling their stock (a capital gain).

Unfortunately, the dynamics of stock ownership are often forgotten when there are thousands of investors buying shares of large companies that are traded in the public markets. All too often, investors are disengaged from the affairs of the underlying business enterprise and become focused exclusively on the current price of the shares they own. Amazingly, many highly-educated, experienced professionals promote the idea that by studying market trends they can predict whether the price of a stock will go up or down. Such a concept defies sound logic and fails to acknowledge the incalculable number of variables that contribute to collective human action. Unlike the movements of heavenly bodies that follow very regular patterns, human beings are not nearly so predictable.

There are indeed some general patterns of behavior that may be predicted with a certain degree of accuracy. For example, when there is a war or global catastrophe the prices of virtually all stocks selling in the market tend to go down temporarily, as people sell and place their funds in financial instruments that they believe will be safer. Or, when there is negative economic news, many investors sell their stocks in the anticipation that the prices will be going down. Their prophecy becomes self-fulfilling. The same phenomenon occurs in the opposite direction when there is positive economic news.

But many investment professionals claim far greater powers of prediction. They believe that by studying the charts and graphs that reflect a stock's recent price history, they can determine it's future price. But any investor following their recommendations would do just as well to solicit the services of a psychic or card reader, as the abilities of such individuals have absolutely no basis in rational methodologies or scientific fact.

Most of the time, the price a stock sells for in the market is completely irrelevant for the prudent investor. When making an initial purchase of stock with accumulated cash, it is important to assess the underlying value of a company as reflected in its share price. Paying too much for a stock at the beginning will significantly diminish your overall returns. There are many metrics and formulas that investment professionals use, but even the average investor with little experience can equip himself to make reasonable decisions by using a few simple valuation tools.

One of the most basic formulas used to determine value is the price/earnings (P/E) ratio. This number is derived by dividing the share price of the stock by the earnings per share during the previous year (the earnings per share are simply the total annual earnings divided by the number of outstanding shares of stock). Thus, a company selling for $20 per share with earnings per share of $2 would have a P/E ratio of 10. This means that you would be paying $10 for every $1 that the company earned. If there were only one company available for sale in the entire world, this number would be completely meaningless. The number is useful because it serves as a basis for comparison with other stocks. If most stocks have higher P/E ratios, say above 15, then a P/E of 10 would represent a stock that is relatively cheap. In general, stocks with P/E ratios below 15 lie at the cheaper end of the spectrum.

But you often get what you pay for. An inexpensive stock may reflect a company with inferior products, services, or management. Nevertheless, purchasing stocks that are expensive (having high P/E ratios) will almost certainly assure inferior returns over the long run. Just as one might search for bargains at auctions or garage sales, a prudent investor should search among the cheaply priced stocks for bargains. A useful tool to help identify them is the Return on Equity (ROE) ratio.

ROE represents the returns a company generates from the invested capital and is a key measure of its efficiency in generating profits. Although calculating the ROE from a company's raw financial data involves a number of steps, the basic idea that it represents is very straightforward. Fishermen are in an excellent position to understand ROE. If a group of them spends a large amount of money to buy a boat and equipment, but doesn't catch very many fish with it year after year, they would probably have been better off just investing the money in Treasury Bills and splitting the interest payments among themselves. Whether an enterprise is established with the funds of one individual or many, it should ultimately provide them with a satisfactory return. An ROE of 15-20 percent is generally considered desirable.

In addition to the money generated by selling stock to investors, most companies will need to take on some debt to fund their operations. However, too much debt can eat up a company's profits just as it can eat up the paycheck of an individual. It also diminishes the value of a company's stock. A homeowner who takes out large home equity loans and additional mortgages will eventually become more of a renter than an owner. The home itself will be almost entirely owned by the bank. In the same way, if you buy stock in a company that is highly leveraged with debt, you really won't be much of an owner. A useful measure of a firm's indebtedness is the Debt/Equity Ratio (D/E), which is derived by dividing the debt by the total number of outstanding shares. A D/E ratio of less than 30 percent is generally considered good.

The ratios above are readily available on the Internet for publicly traded companies. They can usually be found by selecting a detailed stock quote on freely available financial websites. Investors should bear in mind that even when these numbers fall within acceptable ranges, they can be deceptive. Firms can often find ways to manipulate the underlying financial data that they are built upon. Those who are more mathematically inclined may want to make use of the myriad analytical tools that investment professionals have devised to try to peer into a company's inner workings.

Yet doing so may not offer any more assurance of a sound investment. Focusing too much on individual trees can cause one to miss the forest. The quality of the product or service being sold and its popularity in the marketplace is the most obvious and important factor to consider. Good quality control coupled with sustained earnings growth is usually indicative of good management.

What the company does with its earnings is also very important. Smaller firms that are rapidly expanding will need to use most, if not all, of their earnings to finance growth. Thus, investors should not expect to receive any regular income from their shares. Larger firms, however, should be paying the majority of their earnings out to the shareholders as dividends. This is the rationale for any capitalistic enterprise. If they are not, then prudent investors should look into where the money is being spent. All too often, proceeds that rightfully belong to the shareholders are pillaged by greedy CEOs that claim exorbitant salaries and other forms of compensation. They justify such bloated tribute on the grounds that they are extremely talented and have led their companies to greater profitability and caused the share prices to go up in the marketplace.

But even if a firm were to be blessed with such a super-CEO, investing in it would be unsound. A quality company is made up of many talented team members who all make a significant contribution to its success. A single, highly-paid superstar at the head of a bunch of average workers and managers is indicative of a fragile corporate structure that could collapse at any given moment. The company will lack "institutional inertia." As soon as the all-powerful leader leaves, dies, or becomes involved in a scandal, the company will founder. A solid firm is one that possesses a high degree of institutional knowledge and skill that is broadly distributed among the employees.

Private Stock Offerings

Smaller companies and start-ups offer a better opportunity to observe their inner dynamics, but they have other risks that are even more serious. Buying shares in any company that is not large enough to be traded on the major stock exchanges such as the NYSE and the NASDAQ will often result in a complete loss of one's investment.

Venture capitalists, who make it their business to seek out promising new companies to invest in, have a reputation for being ruthless—and with good reason. They know very well that most new businesses—no matter how promising they look in the beginning—will probably fail.

Promising ideas are even worse. It is almost certain that they will never successfully make the jump from invention to commercialization. The U.S. patent office is filled with millions of great ideas that never materialized. Many of them had the potential to really improve our lives, but alas, they were never transformed into a product or service that finally reached the marketplace. Perhaps the founder or inventor couldn't find the money to get started. Maybe he couldn't source the right raw materials at the right price, or find skilled workers and managers to ramp up production. One can only wonder how our lives might have been changed had these wonderful ideas not ended up in the graveyard.

Venture capitalists know more about what might have been than anyone else, except perhaps for the patent clerks themselves. They sift through literally hundreds of proposals every year. These are not back-of-the-envelope ideas pitched by some enthusiastic inventor. A proposal at this stage of development wouldn't even raise an eyebrow—if an aspiring entrepreneur were even fortunate enough to gain an audience with a venture capitalist, which he wouldn't. They aren't interested in great ideas—only in established companies that are already making money.

The founders of these companies must present highly detailed business plans showing exactly how and when they will expand. They must compete with hundreds of other contenders for the coveted investment funds, and they must ultimately be willing to cede the legal control of their enterprises to the venture capitalists if they do not meet certain milestones for sales and growth. After sifting through so many candidates, venture capital firms typically select less than a dozen to receive funding. Of these, they only expect one or two to be successful.

If these are the odds faced by professionals who have the opportunity to compare and contrast so many businesses that are already making money, an individual investor approached by a family member or friend stands little chance of selecting the next early stage Apple Computer company. Usually, there is no selection process at all—just one company and one opportunity to invest. But the ideas can be quite captivating; their promoters so sincere and enthusiastic; and the potential for huge profits so alluring.

Those who are willing to part with their hard earned savings to give an entrepreneur a shot at success are even called "angels." Angel investors, unlike the mean, calculating venture capitalists, are willing to provide seed capital for a good idea—before an operating company even exists. But if a family member or friend truly wants to be an angel, he should just give the money away. That way, when the new venture fails (which it almost certainly will) there will be no hard feelings.

Virtually any startup company will burn through cash like a windblown grass fire. Angel investors who got in at the ground level with a substantial ownership interest will soon be asked to pony up more money to keep the venture going. If they can't or won't, the entrepreneur will seek out other investors who will quickly dilute the shares of the original owners. After just a few stages of financing, a 40 percent ownership interest in a company can soon become 30 percent, 20 percent, and so on. And anything less than 50 percent is completely meaningless, as these investors will have absolutely no decision-making power. Unless everything is clearly spelled out in the beginning in a legal contract, the entrepreneur can elect to retain any earnings for expansion virtually forever, or pay himself an ever-increasing salary.

The only hope for cashing in and making a profit will be an acquisition by a larger company or an initial public offering of stock (IPO). An acquiring company will have absolutely no interest in providing for the original investors. They will make every attempt to get rid of them in the most expedient, cost-efficient way that is still legal. This is often accomplished by providing handsome rewards for the entrepreneur in exchange for his complicity. Those who shared his glorious vision in the beginning will watch it fade away along with their hopes for enormous riches. In the end, any return they make on their investment will probably be far less than what they would have earned on something much safer. All the risk will have been for nothing.

They may fare better in an initial public offering of the company's stock. If a private enterprise ever makes it through the long and arduous process to reach this stage of development, the initial investors can finally cash out. Investment banks will work hard to determine a price for the stock that will provide the greatest possible return for the original investors (and the highest possible commission for the investment bank). They will use their network of brokers to push the stock on their clients, who can often be allured by the same sense of excitement and vision that the private investors once had.

Many will fail to realize that they are coming late to the party, and that all the hype surrounding the launch of the new stock is really designed to maximize the profits of the original investors and the bank. Though occasionally an IPO is a roaring success and the share price rockets skyward on the opening day, most of them quickly fall back down to earth—if they even get off the ground to begin with. Investors will generally do far better if they stick with solid companies whose shares have been well-seasoned by market forces over many years. In this way, it will at least be possible to know that the price has been established by the market itself rather than by the machinations of investment bankers.

Mutual Funds

Many investors are reluctant to engage in the basic analysis necessary to prudently buy stocks. They prefer to leave this task to others whom they perceive to be more qualified. A vast array of mutual funds and hedge funds are available which, for a fee, will relieve investors of this responsibility. But nothing is gained by handing over the decision about which stock to buy to someone else. First of all, the investor will have to pay for this service, which will eat into any of the proceeds from the underlying stocks. Secondly, the investor will no longer have access to any meaningful tools of analysis. Instead of P/E, ROE, D/E ratios and other metrics, prospective investors will only have historical performance data on the fund itself, which is virtually useless for gauging the fund's future performance. Instead of deciding between the stocks of companies with established profits, an investor must now decide between people—and assess their knowledge, skill, and integrity from promotional materials and the comments of financial writers. In the end, a decision about which mutual fund or hedge fund to buy will be more difficult and less objective than a decision about which stock to buy.

Diversification and Dividends

Mutual funds do indeed offer the advantage of spreading risk over a number of stocks, so that if any single company fails or performs poorly all will not be lost. But anyone who decides to invest in individual stocks can easily replicate this advantage simply by buying a variety of them. A reasonable degree of safety can be attained by buying shares of companies that are large, have been around for a long time, and produce products and services that are familiar to the investor. They should also be spread among different industries so that if a certain sector of the economy suffers a decline, all of the stocks will not be affected. It is always a good sign when a stock pays a dividend. As long as the dividend is sustainable, it demonstrates that the company is making money and that it is using the money responsibly.

Comparisons between companies can be made by looking at their Dividend Yields (DY). This number is calculated by dividing the annual dividends per share by the share price. Thus, a company that pays $1 per share in annual dividends and whose shares currently sell for $20 per share will have a DY of 5 percent. Investors will naturally be drawn toward higher dividend yields, and some companies may try to lure people into buying their stock by bumping up dividends to unsustainable levels. Any company that pays out more in dividends than it is actually earning will not be around for long.

The near-term sustainability of a dividend can be checked by comparing a stock's Dividend Rate (DR) to the Earnings Per Share (EPS). The DR is the total dividend amount per share. A company that earns $1 per share during the year but pays out $1.50 per share in dividends cannot continue to do this for long. Sometimes, though, firms that are financially solid may have an established dividend payout rate but have non-recurring costs that temporarily cause the dividends to be more than the earnings per share.

Index Funds

Another way for investors to avoid analyzing individual stocks is to buy shares in an index fund. These funds purchase shares of all the stocks that are tracked by a particular market index. One of the most well known indices, the Dow Jones Industrial Average, tracks 30 of America's largest companies. The S&P 500 is a broader index that tracks 500 firms. Broader still are the Russell 2000 and the Wilshire 5000 indices. There are also some that track foreign stocks or stocks within a particular industry.

Index funds use computers to buy of all of the stocks within a particular index, weighting the share purchases of each company according to its market capitalization. The most popular index funds are based on the S&P 500, the Russell 2000, and the Wilshire 5000 stock indices. Since these funds buy everything listed, they purchase the good along with the bad. The advantage is that they do not have to employ highly paid managers who must spend time analyzing individual stocks. This cost savings is significant, and year after year index funds tend to outperform over eighty percent of active money managers.

When an index is based on the stocks of a particular country, the overall prosperity and economic growth of that nation will have a considerable effect on the performance of the companies the index tracks. If the economy is stagnating, firms will sell fewer goods and services to the populace and profitability will suffer. Multinational corporations that can make substantial profits overseas will be insulated to some extent, but not forever.

During the Peloponnesian War, the great city-state of Athens was engaged in an extended conflict with Sparta. The Spartans possessed a superior land army and eventually overran the Athenians' territory, burning their fields and laying siege to the city itself. The Athenians, however, had a superior naval force and were able to continually resupply their besieged city from their vast network of prosperous overseas colonies. But in the long run, the city fell. Stagnation at home could not be overcome by links to prosperity in faraway places.

During the post WWII years, the United States prospered more than any nation in history. There were seemingly endless opportunities for American businesses. Citizens' incomes rose and they purchased the goods and services that these companies produced. Foreigners were just as eager to buy things produced in America, as there was not much competition from the other industrialized nations. Europe and Japan took many years to recover from the devastation of the war. Even when they did, America had a huge head start that gave it an advantage in developing industries like electronics, computers, and telecommunications.

The Golden Age of American Business lasted until the beginning of the 21st century. During those years, any investor who purchased shares in an index fund was assured of a good return. Buying shares in an index fund such as the S&P 500 was like buying shares in America itself—and it still is. But, sadly, America is a very different place today. Much of the nation's production has been moved overseas—good for the corporate bottom line in the short run but not in the long run. High paying factory jobs in heavy industry have virtually disappeared, and they are quickly vanishing even in the high tech and computer industries.

The average American worker doesn't make very much money any more, and therefore has limited disposable income with which to buy the goods and services that American companies produce. Many of the products that they do buy are made overseas. To make matters worse, they are often bought on credit—an unsustainable practice that will only force these consumers to drastically reduce their purchases at some point in the future. Thus, even the profits that American companies make by marketing foreign products will eventually be compromised.

And now these foreigners have become direct competitors. They already control much of the means of production. Karl Marx described in great detail how control over the means of production gave the bourgeoisie (owners of capital) power over the proletariat (the workers). For many years, Americans downplayed the economic impact of off-shoring their factories, claiming that foreigners lacked creative ability. They could do the dirty grunt work in the overseas sweatshops while the real brainpower remained here at home. Americans were not losing out to foreign competition by shifting production offshore. They were simply moving up the food chain.

But the foreigners residing on other landmasses were never less competent than the foreigners that had blended into the American melting pot to form our own population. To be sure, those who came here benefited greatly from good government, personal freedom, and a body of laws that protected individual property rights. But the American model is now emulated in many other places, empowering people who are just as competent and driven as we are. Many of the nations that were "newly industrializing" in the 1970s and 1980s are now completely industrialized—and in some ways more so than America itself. They, too, want to sell their products and services to the world. And they are doing it—and doing it quite well—sustained by prolific research and development, efficient production, effective quality control, and dedicated management.

Now, back to index funds. Investment companies that market such products typically cite their superior performance over active money managers during the past few decades. But it must be remembered that this performance was in large part a reflection of the overall American economy. If, as the politicians say, the Golden Age of American Business will get a reboot (by printing lots of money and spending it on wars and a potpourri of government-funded projects), then index funds will be a very sound investment.

However, if America must in fact face a day of reckoning for its unbridled government and consumer spending, lack of emphasis on education, and the atrophy of its skilled workforce, buying stock in America by buying an index fund is probably not a good investment decision. Some will deride this advice as unpatriotic, but there are other, more prudent ways to express support for the American system. An impoverished citizenry will only weaken the fabric of the nation and lead to a degradation of its cherished services and institutions.

During WWII, the government urgently needed funds to buy military hardware and pay its soldiers. Since most of the other industrialized nations were embroiled in the war as well, there was no country that had the means to give us a loan. The government therefore turned to its own citizens, asking them to buy war bonds. Surprisingly, even though the country was in the midst of the Great Depression, the American people showed their loyalty by anteing up and buying vast quantities of these bonds. So where did they get the money? Even though scores of people were homeless and hungry, many others had savings. They had lived frugally and accumulated considerable wealth—not the enormous wealth of the Robber Barons of a previous era—they were not all Rockefellers or Vanderbilts or Astors— just regular middle-class Americans, but they had accumulated relative wealth. They were much wealthier than they would have otherwise been had they spent their surplus income on electronics, video games, and tennis shoes. Instead of large amounts of credit card debt (there were none in those days), they had savings. And the nation was able to draw upon the financial strength of its citizens in a time of dire need.

How things have changed! The federal government is completely bankrupt and prints money to pay its skyrocketing bills. The states are bankrupt and are firing teachers and shutting down state parks. Cities are bankrupt and are firing policemen and firemen. Those that risked their lives for decades and passed up opportunities for more lucrative employment in the private sector (with the understanding that they would at least have a decent pension) are now being told that their pensions are going to be re-negotiated because there is no money to pay them. The legal enforcement of contracts (even those that may have been disadvantageous for one of the parties that signed them) is being abandoned as one of the hallmarks of the American free enterprise system. As a response to these frightening economic developments, many Americans are doing what generations of people throughout history have done during times of great uncertainty—they are purchasing gold.

Commodities

As an investment vehicle, gold and other precious metals are classified within a broader category called commodities. A commodity can be any physical item such as a metal or agricultural product. Precious metals, though they may be classified as commodities, have some inherent differences and will therefore be addressed subsequently. Commodity products such as wheat, oil, or pork bellies cannot function as investments for the average person, since they are perishable or have high storage costs. Investors who enter the commodities markets would do just as well to walk into a casino. Like their Vegas counterparts, the commodities markets offer a great variety of games for people to play, such as betting on the future price of a food item. Those who bet on the outcomes of sports matches often spend enormous amounts of time studying facts about the players or the team, thinking that this information will help them outwit those betting against them. Likewise, commodities speculators often know quite a lot about the item they are interested in, be it wheat, soybeans, oil. etc.

The problem in any betting arena, however, is that there are always too many unknown variables that intervene to produce unexpected outcomes. One might argue that, given the relentless pressure of inflation, the prices of virtually any commodity will eventually go up, potentially making it a better hedge than cash stored in a savings account. This is certainly true, but any gains will probably be offset by storage costs. Perishable items like wheat must be consumed quickly, eliminating the possibility of long-term physical possession. But futures contracts sold in the marketplace also expire rather quickly, eliminating the possibility of a long-term claim on a commodity.

Precious metals such as gold have some similar drawbacks, but they also offer other possibilities for investors. Governments as well as the financial industry generally try to discourage people from buying gold. This is quite understandable. Buying gold sucks the lifeblood out of the economy. When people choose to sock away their surplus wealth in the form of something that has virtually no utility—rather than invest their funds in the financial markets to provide capital for economic growth—the national economy suffers.

Financial professionals, many of whom make their living from fees charged to investors, suffer as well. Though a few hedge fund managers are able to charge people to hold their gold for them, most investors want to own the metal outright, locking it away in a home safe or safe deposit box at a bank. Gifted managers are not able to command enormous salaries for their special "gold picking abilities." It is a commodity. It is all the same.

Gold investors are often derided by financial industry professionals as "gold bugs," which gives people the idea that they are pesky little creatures who scurry around in the darker, dirtier fringes of the economy. They are inferior to the mainstream investment community, driven by their irrational fears to hoard a useless metal. Another common ridiculing tactic is to present absurd scenarios of gold owners trying to buy eggs and milk at the grocery store after the economy (and paper currency) has completely collapsed. The standard refrain is that if things get that bad, then gold will be useless anyway.

But things can indeed get that bad, and they have—at various times and places throughout history. When South Vietnam collapsed to the communists after American troops pulled out, many families who were desperate to escape used gold they had saved to bribe communist officials into letting them leave on a massive flotilla of refugee boats. The officials wouldn't accept any of their worthless paper money.

Huy Hoang Nguyen, a mother of two teenage daughters, works as a medical professional in California. She makes it a regular practice to take some of her savings and buy gold coins. When she was eleven years old, communist forces invaded her homeland in South Viet Nam. Her father, who had worked as a special agent for the South Vietnamese army, knew he would be executed if he were captured. He fled with his family to the farm of a relative, where they hid for a year. The family had been steadily accumulating gold on the black market and eventually they were able to use it to pay the captain of a fishing boat to help them escape. Unfortunately, they ended up adrift deep in the Pacific Ocean.

They were finally spotted by a passing ship, but as fate would have it, the ship was Cuban and it was heading straight for Viet Nam. Once again, they were able to use their gold to pay the sailors to drop them off in Singapore. From there, they were sponsored by an aid organization to travel to Turkey and later to Italy and the United States.

Americans will probably never have to use gold to cross the border into Canada or Mexico or pay a fishing boat captain to transport them to Europe or Australia. And gold will probably never become an accepted medium of exchange in a post-apocalyptic American grocery store. Nevertheless, it will always store more value than paper and there will always be someone who will be willing to buy it, trade for it, or make change.

When mockery alone fails to discourage people from buying gold, Wall Street spokespeople present more rational arguments. They show statistics demonstrating gold's poor performance as an investment vehicle during the past few decades of America's Golden Age of Business. And they are quite right. Gold was indeed a poor hedge against inflation. There was little demand for it when the stock market performed so much better. Thus, prices remained low. The unspoken assumption is that the next few decades will not be any different.

Even though the value of gold may shoot up during difficult economic times, it should not be viewed as a conventional investment to cash in on when the price is high. As with stocks, correctly timing the market will be impossible. Rather, gold should be viewed as an insurance policy against a severe and prolonged economic crisis. When such events occur, paper assets like stocks, bonds, and currency can suffer drastic devaluations or even become worthless. Banks can fail and unemployment can skyrocket. Because of its scarcity and its universal appeal as a store of value since ancient times, gold has never once become completely worthless or lost its acceptance as a medium of exchange. Based on this precedent, it has gained a well-deserved reputation as a safe asset to have when everything else is going down the toilet.

Therefore, placing some gold in one's investment portfolio is not at all imprudent. Once purchased, gold should be kept in a safe place until it is absolutely needed, which will hopefully be never. Gold is analogous to those life jackets and oxygen masks on airplanes that never seem to get used. But it is better to have them and not need them than to need them and not have them.

In his 2010 Annual Report To Shareholders, Warren Buffett tells a story about his grandfather, a hardworking grocery store owner who was adamant about saving money and avoiding debt. Believing that it was always prudent to have some cash stashed away in case of an emergency, he began a savings fund for each of his four children on the day that they were married. Each year he would take some money and place it in an envelope until, after ten years, he had reached a sum of $1000. He then presented a sealed envelope full of cash to each of his children, encouraging them to place it in a safe deposit box in a bank.

In an accompanying letter he encouraged them to avoid the temptation to invest the money in something that would bring an income, claiming that the "mental satisfaction" of having $1000 set aside and readily available was worth far more than any interest payments. Mr. Buffett's grandfather was indeed a wise man, and in 1939 when he made the gift to his youngest son, the prospect of holding onto American paper money for a long period of time was much better than it is today. Gold was illegal anyway.

Warren Buffett became the executor of his aunt's estate in 1970 and when he opened her safe deposit box, he found his grandfather's letter to his uncle, along with the envelope of cash that had been faithfully preserved all of those years. By that time, however, each of those 1939 dollars was worth only 36 cents, as measured by their purchasing power. The entire $1000 would have been required to buy what $360 would have purchased in 1939. If Warren Buffett had decided to use the money to pay for his aunt's funeral expenses, he would have had to use virtually all of it (the average cost of a funeral in 1970 was around $983). Yet in 1939 this service would have cost about $350.

If Mr. Buffet's grandfather had been able to purchase $1000 worth of gold at the 1939 price of $35 per ounce (a price artificially fixed by the United States government), it would have been worth only $36.02 in 1970. At this time, the international price of gold was still largely controlled by the United States. Thus, 28 ½ ounces of gold purchased in 1939 could have been sold in 1970 for $1026.57. The $26.57 would not even have been sufficient to cover the commission for the sale of the metal. If, however, his aunt had lived just a few more years, until the end of 1973 when the United States abandoned its policy of trying to fix an artificial price for gold, those 28 ½ ounces would have sold at the new market-based price of $120 per ounce. Their sale would have generated $3420. The funeral would have cost around $1059.

Thus, the proportion of the total savings required to pay for the service of the funeral would have been about the same as it would have been in 1939. Paper currency stashed away for an emergency will provide little peace of mind if its value is drastically eroding year after year. Gold, on the other hand, offers some security in the face of inflation.

When gold prices have skyrocketed, as they have in recent years, a lot of people are reluctant to make a purchase for fear that the price will go back down again. It probably will. And it will go back up again, and back down again, and so on and so on. No one can predict what the price of gold will do in the short term, so purchase decisions should be made on the basis of targeted goals for one's portfolio rather than on expectations about price.

In the 1986 movie *Star Trek IV: The Voyage Home* there is a robotic alien probe that is about to destroy Earth. Mr. Spock figures out that the probe's signals match the songs of Humpback whales, which have long since become extinct in the earth's oceans. They decide that the only way to save the planet is to travel into the past and bring a pair of these giant creatures back to the future, in the hope that they will be able to communicate with the probe and send it away. By employing a high-speed slingshot maneuver around the sun, they are able to travel back in time to Earth in the 1980s.

They land in San Francisco, where their unusual uniforms from the future fail to elicit even a casual glance from passersby. Unfortunately, they have no money at all, which they desperately need to pay for basic expenses as they set about figuring out how to bring back a couple of whales that are being held in an aquarium at a local ocean study institute. Captain Kirk eventually realizes that he has with him an old pocket watch that has been handed down to him from his family through many generations. He presents the watch to a pawnbroker and asks how much he will pay him for it. The pawnbroker inspects it and replies somewhat tentatively, "a hundred dollars?" Captain Kirk then asks him, "Is that a lot?"

If Kirk had been can economic historian rather than a starship captain, he would have been able to ascertain about how much $100 dollars represented in terms of its purchasing power and relative value for people living nearly three hundred years before he was born. It is indeed possible to look at past prices and make comparisons with prices for similar goods at different points in history and determine whether they were higher or lower.

But even when the present price of gold or any other commodity is extremely high compared with prices in the past, it might turn out to have been rather low once it becomes possible to compare it with future prices. When it comes to assessing the current price of gold, we will all find ourselves in the position of Captain Kirk, having to ask ourselves, "Is that a lot?" There is simply no way to know until we travel further into the future. But for the long term, there is reasonable assurance that no matter how many dollars you spend to buy a certain quantity of gold, it will be worth many more of them far down the road. And there is little chance that this metal will one day become completely worthless.

There are a number of ways for investors to own gold, some of which defeat the very purpose of owning it in the first place. Recently, gold exchange traded funds have become available in the stock market, so that people can conveniently purchase shares of gold through their brokerage accounts just like they would buy a stock. But they are really just buying another paper asset, since they never take direct ownership of the metal. They would be better off buying shares of profitable companies, which would probably perform much better. Owning a claim on gold that is supposedly held for you by a Wall Street firm is about as good as owning a claim on gold in a faraway mine that you have never seen. If you really needed the gold during an economic crisis, you might find out that it was never really there to begin with, or that it quickly disappeared once the crisis began.

An even worse way to own gold is to pay a slick investment manager to buy it and keep it for you in his hedge fund, all the while charging you enormous fees for the service. Many people have been lured into such schemes, believing that some genius will know just when to sell so they can cash in on the profits. Once again, the very purpose of owning gold to begin with is utterly defeated.

If you fear a government confiscation and want to keep the metal overseas, you will have no choice but to contract the services of a secure storage company. There are a number of such companies that are quite large and that have been in business for many years. This option may be desirable for at least some of the gold holdings of very wealthy individuals. The downside is that there will be moderate fees, which will slowly erode the value of the holdings. The Perth Mint in Australia is a government-backed institution that sells gold and allows investors to keep it in their vaults without charging a fee.

Ultimately, there is no substitute for having physical possession of the metal itself. A bank safe deposit box or home safe is generally a good option for self storage. The danger of theft can be minimized by using a safe with the highest protection rating (TL-30) and keeping it hidden from view. Buying gold in bar form is cheaper than coins, but it can be problematic if an investor ever wants to sell. Once a bar is taken out of the dealer network, it can no longer be relied upon for purity, as anyone could remove a core of metal from the interior of the bar or even fabricate a counterfeit bar by coating a cheaper metal with a gold veneer. Gold-covered tungsten bars that had the correct weight and appearance have been discovered in China and Germany. For this reason, investors who want to sell back their gold bars will have to get them assayed first.

Government-minted 1oz. coins, such as American Buffalos or Eagles, Canadian Maple Leafs, Austrian Philharmonics, or South African Krugerrands will cost a bit more than an ounce of gold in bar form, but they are readily accepted by any gold dealer. Their authenticity can be verified simply by weighing them on a digital scale.

A primary concern for anyone investing in gold is that it might once again be confiscated by the U.S. government. It is difficult to imagine that citizens could really be forced to turn in their gold holdings, but a precedent has already been established. The executive order of 1933 allowed for some exceptions, notably collectable coins that in addition to their gold content possessed numismatic value. Numismatic value is usually derived from the historical nature of a coin, and varies drastically depending on its condition and rarity. Rare coins receive grades from experienced numismatists that help determine the price they will sell for in the marketplace. But such assessments are more art than science and can vary considerably. For this reason, it is very difficult to determine exactly how much a collectable coin is worth. Price is ultimately determined by how much a buyer is willing to pay. Someone who really wants a certain coin because he needs it to complete his collection may be willing to pay far more than someone else.

It would have been a logistical nightmare for the U.S. government to take on the role of assessing the fair market value of peoples' collectable coins in 1933, as it would be today. The "Eminent Domain" clause found in the Fifth Amendment to the U.S. Constitution does indeed allow the government to confiscate any of its citizens' property if it is for the good of the country. This would probably not be too difficult to prove if the government were bankrupt and the country were in the midst of a severe economic crisis—as it was in 1933. But the Constitution also states that citizens must be compensated for their confiscated property at fair market value. Because of the difficulty in assessing this value for collectable gold coins, they were spared in 1933.

Gold investors who have bought coins with numismatic value as insurance against confiscation are hoping that they would once again be spared if history repeats itself. But there is more than one way to skin a cat. Rather than force people to turn in their gold, the government could levy a tax on it similar to an intangibles tax that some states have imposed on peoples' financial assets. Citizens could be required to have all of their collectable gold coins assessed by government-licensed numismatists, and then pay an annual tax on their total value.

Thus, if an economic crisis becomes too severe, there will be no safe havens. Nevertheless, some investors might want to establish an extra level of security by purchasing some collectable gold coins. If they are inexperienced, they will need the services of a trusted expert, as it is extremely easy to get burned in these markets. A simpler solution would be to purchase "proof" or commemorative gold coins directly from the U.S. Mint, which are already classified as collectables.

There will be a premium over the price paid for bullion, but the added peace of mind may be worth it for some.

Investors who do not have the resources to purchase gold might opt instead for silver, which can also function as a store of value. However, its price is much more volatile and it will be more difficult to store if purchased in large quantities. As with gold, coins are the better option, since in the mind of the buyer a shiny silver bar could be made from any number of cheaper metals with a similar appearance. Precious metals should never comprise the lion's share of one's portfolio, since they are inherently inferior to other investment vehicles like stocks. A conservative recommendation would be about 5 percent. Larger allocations lose touch with a prudent "insurance" rationale and become speculation.

Real Estate

For many people, real estate is more appealing than other types of investments that are less tangible. Traditionally, fertile farmland was always a valuable asset. If used productively, it could provide a good living for the farmer and his family. Throughout the late 19th century and early 20th centuries, a growing number of Americans moved into the cities, lured by high factory wages and the prospect of a better life. In 1913 Henry Ford began a revolution by offering an unheard of $5-a-day wage for anyone willing to come and work in his auto factory. Other manufacturers had no choice but to raise their wages as well, and more and more people abandoned farming as a way of life.

Fortunately, agriculture was becoming more mechanized, so that fewer people were needed to provide food for the nation. Now, less than 5 percent of the American population makes a living from farming, yet they not only provide for food needs at home, but for much of the world. Massive mechanized farms are run by large agribusiness firms that employ an army of highly trained specialists to ensure the most productive harvests. Understandably, it has become almost impossible for small, family run farms to compete. A few have carved out a niche for themselves by growing organic produce and selling it in local farmers markets. These individuals would probably have the knowledge and experience to make good investments in farmland.

But the vast majority of the population would be at a tremendous disadvantage. A few city dwellers have managed to return to the country and establish successful farms or wineries, and the idea is certainly very appealing to many who are tired of the hectic pace of city life. As the economic base of those residing in urban centers continues to erode, there may be an exodus back to the country, where those with savings would have the means to purchase a small farm. They could perhaps raise enough livestock and produce to meet their food needs and possibly even acquire a bit of spending money from sales at the local market. If society were to take such an ironic demographic turn, then those who already know how to farm will have a huge competitive advantage for making valuable real estate purchases. Identifying choice farmland is not a skill easily learned from reading a book.

Previously, the ability to spot the best urban properties was much more lucrative. Many developers made enormous profits by paving over fields and forests to create residential neighborhoods and commercial centers. Urban culture trumped agriculture as cities sprawled into the surrounding countryside, swallowing up what had once been productive farmland. Once these properties acquired municipal status they became far more valuable. Many average people found that they could make quick profits by buying a new house from a developer and then immediately turning around and selling it to someone else.

Others added some value to the sale by finding older homes in existing neighborhoods and fixing them up. These real estate investors discovered that they could easily get loans to make their purchases, even if they had no real means to pay them back. They figured the home would be sold before that ever became necessary anyway. They could take the profits and repeat the process. The banks and lending agencies didn't care about being paid back either, since lots of loans could all be bundled up and sold as interest paying securities to unsuspecting investors. Many of the purchasers of these bogus financial instruments were foreigners, who placed their faith in the strength and integrity of America and the previously untarnished reputation of its credit rating agencies.

But alas, the boom is finally over. A few diehards are still trying to make money on the way down, auctioning troubled loans and guiding bankrupt homeowners through the process of short sales. Buyers sift through properties selling at fraction of their previous cost, thinking that when the market finally recovers they will make a killing. The current real estate market resembles a giant garage sale being held on the deck of the

Titanic. Perhaps a few will be able to make a quick profit before it all goes under, but there is no doubt about where things are headed. People would do well to heed a classic line from the recent movie about the ill-fated ship. When one of the wealthy passengers argues with the chief engineer who built the vessel, claiming that it couldn't possibly sink, the engineer responds: "She's made of iron, sir. I assure you, she will sink. It is a mathematical certainty."

And the future of urban real estate in America seems no less certain. People buy homes in cities when they have jobs and earn enough income to pay for them. When there are no longer any jobs, people eventually have to leave and the properties they lived and worked in become abandoned. The numerous ghost towns scattered across the western United States are a testimony to this stark reality. When the mines stopped producing, people had to leave. They couldn't all stick around and sell hamburgers to each other. Those who doubt that this can really happen need only watch the process occurring in real-time in places like Detroit.

There will always be exceptions that will provide opportunities to make a profit in urban real estate. But the fundamental principle on which this book is based is that people who want to accumulate wealth should focus on what is general rather than on what is exceptional. A few cities may experience a renewal based on some as yet unforeseen new industry. Many are currently pinning their hopes on green technology. But without the robust economies that built them, today's metropolises are unsustainable.

Rural real estate will perhaps experience a boom as the global need for food increases and arable land becomes scarcer. Scientists have been issuing continual warnings about a looming global water crisis and the steady depletion of phosphorus from the topsoil. Agricultural productivity is starting to decline while population continues to grow. The future result of these trends is not hard to predict. But cashing in on this calamity by buying up good farmland will be very difficult for greenhorn city dwellers. Perhaps a few who have friends or relatives out on the farm will be able to form lucrative partnerships.

Chapter 8

Conclusion:
The Future Of Wealth Creation In America

A nation's economic salvation does not lie in the amount of money its rich inhabitants can squander recklessly. A nation's economic salvation lies in the amount of money its inhabitants can save and invest after providing themselves with all the necessaries and all the reasonable comforts of life.

—R. C. Forbes

As seen at the beginning of this book, people have always created wealth by engaging in four broad categories of economic activities: growing food, collecting useful raw materials to make things with, making things, and providing services to other people. Nothing has changed in thousands of years of human history. Our primitive ancestors, not unlike their animal counterparts lower down on the food chain, realized that certain geographical regions facilitated or hindered this process. Areas with plenty of water, forests, and a good climate were highly coveted, and both people and animals were often willing to fight to control them. As humans became more civilized, their interests extended beyond good watering holes and hunting grounds. Even empty desert quarters could hold rich deposits of metals or valuable minerals like salt. Riches could be gained by trading these items to people living in different territories who possessed other valued commodities.

Again, nothing has changed. Saudi Arabia is, for the most part, an empty desert wasteland. But beneath its scorching sands lies a treasure that is coveted by all the nations of the world. By selling its oil, Saudi Arabia has not only been able to meet the water and food needs of its people, it has provided them with a comparatively high standard of living, complete with a good medical services, public infrastructure, and educational opportunities.

Haiti, on the other hand, is not so fortunate. Although the island is located in the tropics, much of its territory bears some resemblance to a desert wasteland. Most of the trees have been cut down to create farmland. Unfortunately, the fields thus created are no longer productive because much of the fertile soil has now eroded into the ocean. These once pristine Caribbean waters have now become clouded with topsoil, which has ruined the fishing. All along, the population of this tiny island has exploded. There are now millions of people trapped there who have no good way to make a living. There is no good land to farm; there are no minerals or oil in the ground; and most of the workers are unskilled and have no prospect of manufacturing anything that the rest of the world wants. Their only real prospect is to provide services to each other. A few political leaders are able to prosper by taxing the meager revenues of the citizens; doctors can eek out a living by providing medical services; and church leaders and voodoo practitioners can be sustained by their followers.

The prospects of becoming wealthy in Haiti are nearly impossible. Nevertheless, industrious individuals will always have the potential to achieve relative wealth—and this is the best that anyone can really hope for no matter where they live. Of course, the relative wealth of an average American will be many times greater than that of an average Haitian. But in the future it might not be nearly as great as that of a citizen of some other nation that has become productive and implemented sound financial policies. Americans have grown accustomed to being the richest people in the world, a position that they enjoyed for many decades. But in spite of the political rhetoric, this condition cannot possibly continue. Indeed, the change is taking place very rapidly in the wake of the recent financial crisis.

A high standard of living can no longer be assured just by residing in this particular region of

North America. Many of the resources have been exhausted, global warming threatens the bread basket of the Midwest, manufacturing has moved to other places, and many who had sought refuge in the service sector have discovered—much to their dismay—that it is already very crowded. The thousands of displaced workers pouring into this sector can't all make a living by selling houses to each other anymore.

But it must be remembered that making a living—and especially acquiring wealth—has always been hard. Over the centuries, various civilizations emerged that succeeded in generating relative wealth for the majority of their citizens. That is, they lived better than most of the people in most other places. Americans have enjoyed their day in the sun, and on that day it shined more brightly that at any point in all of human history. A middle-class American was able to enjoy comforts and luxuries that a Roman emperor could never have even dreamed of.

Try as we might—and we should—we cannot control the destiny of the political and economic system that we are bound up with. But as long as we are free—and fortunately in America we still are—we can indeed exercise a great amount of control over our individual destinies.

About The Author

Foster Stanback is a managing partner at various domestic and international firms engaged in business activities that include shipping, distribution, retail sales, and real estate. He has been an active investor in international equities markets for over two decades. He holds an M.A. in Sociology from Florida Atlantic University, where he received a distinguished alumnus award in 2011. He also holds an M.A. in Religion from Pepperdine University, an M.A. in Psychology from the Pepperdine Graduate School of Education and Psychology, and an M.S. in Marketing and Technology Innovation from the Worcester Polytechnic Institute. In 2010 he was inducted into the Beta Gamma Sigma International Honor Society for Collegiate Schools of Business.

www.ingramcontent.com/pod-product-compliance
Lightning Source LLC
Chambersburg PA
CBHW060902170526
45158CB00001B/465